British Council of Churches
Consultative Group
on
Ministry among Children

Reports of the Working Parties on
THE CHILD IN THE CHURCH
AND
UNDERSTANDING
CHRISTIAN NURTURE

Cover illustration: Freddie Hobbs aged 5 years
of Dulwich Village Infants School, South London.

Acknowledgements: All biblical quotations are from the Revised Standard
Version. © 1946 and 1952 Division of Christian Education, National Council
of Churches of Christ in the USA.

Part One first printed 1976
Part Two first printed 1981
New combined edition fully revised 1984

ISBN 0-85169-180-3

CONTENTS

Preface by the Revd Dr Philip Morgan
General Secretary British Council of Churches

PART ONE: THE CHILD IN THE CHURCH

PART TWO: UNDERSTANDING CHRISTIAN NURTURE

PREFACE

The constant demand for our two reports, *The Child in the Church* (1976) and its successor *Understanding Christian Nurture* (1981) have prompted this new and combined edition, revised to take account of certain changes over the years, although the texts remain substantially the same. All that has happened in the churches since the first report was issued has served to confirm the importance of the topic and the urgency of the concern. We still need to take the children of the Church much more seriously, both to fulfil our obligation to nurture them in the Christian faith, and to learn from them as a total church community. This book places on parents and on the Church a prime responsibility for Christian nurture over and above any Christian education or nurture to be found in our schools. It also explores the distinction between nurture and education, and calls for critical openness against a background of assured faith. The detailed examination of this issue in the second report is of great importance in developing Christian education at all ages and in both formal and informal ways. I hope that this new edition will continue to stimulate the development of our ministry with children to the enrichment of us all.

PHILIP MORGAN

General Secretary, British Council of Churches

Some people were going to Church. They heard the sound of the bell. - Thomas Quilter 5 yrs

Chapter 1
BACKGROUND

1. The present British situation of the child in the Church must be seen in relation to changes which have taken place in the last two hundred years or so. In seventeenth century Britain, most Christian nurture of children took place in the home and through the extended family of god-parents. It involved knowing something of the teachings of the church and especially the morality which was thought to flow from that teaching. It also involved attendance at public worship. The catechisms were an important aid, offering to parents and clergy an outline of question and response concerning Christian faith and life.

2. This pattern began to break down in the eighteenth century because of the rise of the factory system, the vast increase in urban population, and the decay of the medieval parish structure. A tendency appeared for children to be gathered together in groups, usually in homes, for the purpose of religious instruction, and sometimes instruction in reading. Under the influence of Robert Raikes, this led to the birth of the Sunday School movement. The immense popularity of this may be attributed to the fact that there was, before the creation of the school systems of the early nineteenth century, little competition from other educational bodies, and the commodity offered (reading and writing plus Christian morality) was in great demand. This may be contrasted with the situation of the Church's educational ministry to children on Sundays at the present time, which is taking place in a highly competitive situation, and which offers something not in great demand — initiation into Christian faith in an age of secularism and pluralism.

3. It seems unlikely that the children in the Sunday School movement were ever thought of as being 'children in the Church' in the sense which is implied in the title of this Report. Very few indeed of these children joined the church as a result of their experiences in the Sunday School. By the end of the nineteenth century, the Sunday morning school (and thus attendance at Church on Sunday morning) had declined very seriously. In many churches the afternoon service of worship had moved to the evening as a result of 'gas lighting' and so the church building was used increasingly by various groups of people meeting at different times, and leaving the children isolated from other groups. In the early twentieth century, a series of conferences and reports investigated this situation. The grading of classes was found to be seldom satisfactory, the teaching frequently dull and unimaginative, and the use of the bible often unintelligent. These have been the perennial problems of the church's work with children for seventy-five years.

4. The situation today presents some features which are strikingly similar (like the ones just noted) and others which are new and different. On the whole, the children who came in contact with the church through the schools on Sunday in the eighteenth and nineteenth centuries were working class children and came without their parents. Today, the children in the Churches

1

tend (with many exceptions) to be from middle class homes, and to attend with one or both parents. Almost all Churches report a decline in the numbers of children and young people in attendance, whether at public worship or in one of the church-related organizations. Attendance appears to decrease after pupils reach the age of ten to twelve years, but in some areas children are already leaving by the age of nine.

5. The Working Party has examined evidence, presented in written and verbal form, from many Churches and individuals (see Appendix). The following general trends appear to be significant.

(a) All Church bodies are concerned with the quality of the teachers or the group leaders. Considerable effort is being devoted to teacher training through courses, conferences and other assistance. In many cases, these provisions are on an ecumenical basis (see Recommendation 4). The headquarters of most Churches offer correspondence courses for workers with children, and agencies such as the Methodist Church Division of Education and Youth, the National Council of Christian Education, Bishop Otter College in Chichester and Westhill College in Birmingham offer full or part time courses leading to a Certificate or a Diploma in Religious or Christian Education. (see Recommendation 1).

(b) Lesson materials for pupils have changed considerably in the past ten years and are still a matter of constant concern and redevelopment by all churches. The British Lessons Council's syllabus of 1968 *Experience and Faith* and the *Partners in Learning* materials based on it have been influential, and a new four year syllabus, more closely related to the lectionary approved for use in all the Churches, is approaching completion. The Anglican material *Alive in God's World* has been another notable contribution to curriculum. All the current material is based on the educational value of the actual experience of the child within the Church, taking the Church year and the bible as the main elements of the Church's community life. The use of catechisms is virtually unknown in the Free Churches but continues to some extent in the Anglican and Roman Catholic Churches. The catechisms are presented in a more liberal way, so that the questions and answers are seen to grow out of the experience and insight of the group, the actual wording of the catechism being used as summary of what has already been learned.

(c) Because of the predominance of afternoon Sunday School, the possibilities created by the attendance of children at morning worship were not really faced until the late 1930s and early 1940s, when the Revd. H.A. Hamilton introduced his idea of the Church as a family. Hamilton sought to bring together the Sunday School and the adult church in the opening worship. Children and parents were to sit together, 'Church Friends' being provided for children who came without parents. Active patterns of learning were to be encouraged, the whole Church family was to celebrate together the great festivals of the year, and the Church as a community of learning and caring was to be fostered. There have been a number of denominational variants, but the general concern of the Churches over the past ten years has been to develop further these insights, especially the idea of the Church as a learning community.

(d) In recent years all Churches have had committees or commissions looking at problems of Christian initiation, whether in the form of baptism, membership reception or confirmation. Admission of children to the Lord's Supper, the Holy Communion or the Eucharist is also under active debate. In the Roman Catholic Church, the documents from the Second Vatican Council have sharpened the debate; in the Church of England the growth of the practice of 'Parish Communion' has been the main stimulus; in the Free Churches, ecumenical discussions have brought these questions to the forefront. (see Recommendation 9). The publication by the World Council of Churches of the text *Baptism Eucharist and Ministry* for discussion by the member churches, and its enthusiastic reception in Britain and Ireland confirms the centrality of the questions.

(e) Concern for parent education is part of a growing interest in the problems of adult education within the Churches. It is increasingly being recognised that the educational task of the Church towards children and their parents is one and indivisible. (see Recommendation 3).

(f) Various experiments relating to the nurture and education of children in the Churches have been reported to us. We are not a research group and have not been able to determine whether these few experiments are indicative of a general readiness to adopt new approaches. While we note the good reporting of such innovatory work in periodicals such as *Link* (National Council of Christian Education) and *Together* (Church of England Board of Education) we think that there should be some more thorough ecumenical research project in order to discover, assess and recommend to the churches a variety of new ideas and methods. (see Recommendation 7).

6. The publication of *The Child in the Church* in 1976 has greatly assisted the public debate of these issues. It has been widely read and discussed, not only at national committees, but in local meetings up and down Britain and Ireland. *Understanding Christian Nurture*, published in 1981, took the discussion deeper and further. We republish these two texts together now because they seem to have articulated a concern widely felt in the Christian churches of these islands. Some would say that we face a crisis of Christian nurture. Certainly this is not the first time there has been a crisis, and a study of the history of the child in the Church may suggest that there has never been anything but a series of problems in this area. Nevertheless, the situation of the Christian faith in modern Britain is so precarious, the pace of change is so much greater than before, and the resources of the Churches are so depleted, that our conviction is that without more radical thinking and action in the field of nurture the future of Christian life and faith in Britain is seriously at risk.

7. We are not able to claim that in the course of our many discussions we have agreed upon solutions to these profound problems. But we have tried to make a contribution to the necessary rethinking in the hope that more of our fellow Christians will be encouraged to continue the urgent task of renewal.

Noah's Ark - Kate Royal 5 yrs

4

Chapter 2

GROWING UP IN BRITAIN TODAY:
THE CONTEXT OF CHRISTIAN NURTURE

8. Childhood is experienced differently in different parts of the world. Growing up in America is not the same as growing up in Africa. Coming of age in Spain is not the same as it is in Russia. Even within the British Isles, to be aged twelve is one thing in Belfast, another in rural Shropshire, and another in Surrey.

9. Because growing up is different in different societies, so growing up as a Christian in Victorian England was quite different from the experience of children in Christian homes in this country today. Victorian children's books were not like ours. There was no television. Children experienced the nearness of death more frequently than today. In Britain, society has changed, Christianity has changed, and what it means to mature as a Christian person has also changed.

10. But to a large extent, British Christians have either kept the traditional patterns of Christian upbringing, or are simply abandoning them without finding satisfactory substitutes. This is one important reason why Christian nurture is no longer so effective. What are the main ways in which the situation of the Christian child has changed in recent years? How should these changes effect the way we think about the problem of Christian nurture today?

1. CHANGES IN SOCIETY

11. Families in Britain became much more affluent from 1950 onwards, in particular in the late 1960s and early 1970s. More children than ever before are growing up in homes in which the washing machine, fridge/freezer, video recorder and central heating are taken for granted. Poverty still exists, and relative poverty is increasing with the growth of unemployment. So while in the 1980s about 10 million people a year take their annual holiday abroad another 2 million live with incomes below the short-term rate for supplementary benefit. However, poverty is not the experience of most children. By 1979 67% of households had a telephone, against 32% ten years earlier; 58% of households had a car, 11% had two cars. 53% of householders are owner-occupiers, and this figure continues to increase as council houses are sold. Provisional estimates for 1983 indicated that 25% of households had a video-recorder, and colour television is almost universal. The sale of personal computers in 1983 far exceeded the expectations of the manufacturers. While cinema and football attendances continued to decline in the early 1980s, participation in sport and the home entertainment market continued to increase.

12. Increased affluence, the construction of the motorways, and the increase in car ownership have led to increased mobility. Fewer children now live in the same village or town as their grandparents and their aunts and uncles. The average number of children in each family has tended to decline, and the rapid turnover of population in a given local area has affected not only the experience of community for the child but the pattern of week-end behaviour. More than fifty per cent of week-end 'social motoring' takes place for family visiting. How appropriate are the traditional forms of Sunday observance for these scattered families? How effective can the family be as an agent of Christian nurture in these circumstances?

13. The enormous increase in the availability of information, especially through the mass media, and the changing patterns of leisure behaviour are also affecting the conditions of Christian upbringing. There seems to be a declining interest in passive leisure pursuits outside the home, and an increase in recreations which require active participation. During the last few years garden centres and do-it-yourself shops have flourished, with a great increase of Sunday trading in this sector.

14. But the provisions of the Church, particularly in study and worship, tend to remain rather passive. Adult Christians sit and listen, perhaps they read, they are visited from time to time in their homes. The techniques of communication generally employed by the Church compare rather unfavourably with the variety, the humour, the subtlety and the professionalism which people have learned to expect from the politicians, the advertisers and the entertainers, who compete for their attention in the world outside the Church. Communication in the Church remains largely verbal,and church music too often fails to rival the colour and the vigour of contemporary pop, folk, film and television music. (see paragraph 21).

15. The influx of people from other cultures and from other religions has further contributed to the richness and the diversification of British society. Children in many of our urban schools are in daily contact with those whose family background is Jewish, Muslim, Sikh or Hindu. The Christian way of life is increasingly seen as but one amongst many religious ways, and the religious ways of life increasingly appear as alternatives to the secular outlooks. How does a Christian young person live as a Christian in his school today? What does he learn, directly or indirectly, about his multi-faith society from his school? How does this compare with what he learns about his society from his Church? How, in a society like this, can Christian faith provide him with a learning environment which will be significant in his life?

16. Fundamental changes in authority, convention and ritual confront the child as he grows up in Britain today. The adults around him are now less inclined to accept the authority of the policeman, the teacher, the politician and the clergyman. Inherited conventions of behaviour are widely questioned. That which is new often has a prestige which the old lacks. Age no longer necessarily brings with it greater respect from the young, unless this is seen to be deserved or won by the elderly. The inherited rituals, such

as those associated with courtship and marriage, with patriotism, with meal times and with dying, once provided a framework which expressed the security of a settled community. In a volatile society, where pluralism and affluence make a greater range of life-styles readily available, the old rituals seem less meaningful, and new rituals tend to appear. Fashions in clothing and popular music come and go rapidly, attracting fervent support, while others seem to find a sort of tribal loyalty in following a sporting team or pop group. In contrast, the life and rituals of the Church often seem to speak of a vanished age. Too often the architecture, the moral codes and the language of the Churches strike the young as being quaint and remote. The bible, even to church-going young people, can often appear an alien book, speaking of an antique world into which the modern person can never enter.

2. CHANGES IN OUR UNDERSTANDING OF CHILDHOOD

17. Children, like adults, are people at certain stages of the constant development which takes place between cradle and grave. During the last fifty years there has been a significant growth of our understanding of the characteristics and the sequences of the various stages of human development, a development through which both Christians and non-Christians pass. Our concern, as Christians and as teachers, is to enable the child to achieve his potential wholeness as a person at whatever stage he may be. This will include the Christian relationships and the Christian response appropriate to the child's level of maturity.

18. All processes of nurture, including Christian nurture, assume that the natural potential of the child can be fulfilled or thwarted by the child's environment. Inherited and other physical factors clearly set broad limits to the possibilities of future development, but, as studies of identical twins reared in different circumstances have shown, the human being is extremely adaptable. It is this flexibility, together with the lengthy period of growth before maturity is achieved (which is a feature of the human species) that makes the nurture of the child so significant.

19. (a) *Social development* is crucial to emotional, intellectual, moral and language development. Some homes, for example, may tend to offer the child fewer outside activities and a narrower range of experiences. The vocabulary of these homes may be more restricted. But in other homes parents tend to encourage children to have a greater variety of interests, and may take them on more family outings, which enlarge their vocabulary and their social experience. These children may hear more discussion, more complicated speech patterns, and they read and are read to. Some children may therefore be considerably more mature by the age of five years than others. Although the stages of moral thinking and responding seem to be broadly similar for all children, who all pass through them in the same general order, some children may progress through the stages more rapidly, because of the more stimulating world in which they live.

(b) *Emotional development* is fostered if the child experiences from birth a reliable and loving relationship first with his mother, then with his father, and then with an increasing circle of relations and friends. Self-confidence and a sense of identity are built up through these dependable relationships. The ability to respond to others, to give affection, and to communicate in all sorts of other ways is built up by such early experience, and this forms the basis of later relationships. There apears to be a grim probability that battered babies will grow up to become parents who batter their babies. But in a secure and loving home, set within a familiar routine, a child can gain a sense of history, as familiar events are anticipated, and he comes to see himself as a person with a past, expressed in anecdotes about his past which are told to him. His story becomes his sense of history.

(c) *Intellectual development* also passes through a series of stages, becoming more complex with increased age and experience. The work of the Swiss psychologist, Jean Piaget, has been very influential in religious education, as in many other fields. Piaget observed that children pass from a 'pre-conceptual' stage of thinking, through an 'intuitive' stage to a stage of 'concrete' thinking, finally reaching 'abstract' or 'formal' thinking in early or middle adolescence. Ronald Goldman, in the middle 1960s, applied this finding to the child's religious growth, confirming Piaget's stage theory, and so giving support to the idea that there comes a period in a child's life when he is 'ready' for a more advanced kind of religious thinking. More recent work in the United States has shown that, in America at least, some children may be passing into the abstract stage as early as eight years, but other may be still in the concrete stage as late as fifteen or sixteen years. It would be too hasty to accept, with Goldman, that children are unable to think abstractly about religion much before the age of thirteen or fourteen. We should probably be more adventurous with younger children, and rather more cautious with many adolescents. Although we do not yet have sufficient research results to offer us certain guidance, the work of the last ten or fifteen years has shown that there are characteristic levels of childhood religious understanding, and that teaching is unlikely to be effective unless these are reckoned with.

(d) What is it which encourages the child to develop in all of these interrelated spheres, whether in exploring the world, in language and feelings,or in progressing from one stage of thinking to the next? The crucial factor in motivating development seems to be provided by the quality of the *personal relationship* which surround the child from the earliest period.

20. Aspects of child development have been described which are relevant to the general nurture of all children. How relevant are these considerations for the task of specific Christian nurture? Here are some of the questions which churches might ask themselves, when enquiring into the quality of the Christian nurture they offer.

i How creative, stimulating and challenging is the environment in the Christian community?

ii What concern for the individuality of each child is shown by the Christian community?

iii Do the children see a high quality of relationship in the lives around them in the church?

iv What variety of opportunity for physical involvement in the life and worship of the community is available for children and young people?

v How sensitive is the church to the emotional, social and intellectual capabilities of children?

vi What responsibility does the church exercise towards children who come from deprived backgrounds?

vii How involved is the church in parent education? Are parents helped to interpret their own role towards their children in the light of Christian nurture?

viii Are adults in the church aware of the different levels through which children pass? Is care taken to ensure that the aims, methods and content of Christian education are appropriate to each stage? Is progression to the next stage of thinking encouraged?

ix Are those in the church who work with children and worship in their presence aware of the difficulties which are presented by religious language? Does the church see it as being important to talk and listen to children, so enriching the children's understanding of religious words?

x Is the prime importance of personal relationship in motivating development accepted and operated at every level?

3. CHANGES IN EDUCATION

21. The activity methods increasingly used in the schools are often in contrast with the older methods of some church Sunday programmes. On the other hand, where the Sunday education is based on activity methods, young people sometimes find that they have not been prepared for the passivity still so often expected of them when they join the adult congregation. (see paragraph 14).

22. Other developments in education are changing the world for the growing child. For many years, the county schools have been seen as agents of Christian nurture. School worship and classroom religious education were intended to encourage children in Christian living. But it is now generally recognised that it is unrealistic for the day schools to treat all their pupils as if they are or ought to be Christians. If the schools are to encourage Christian faith, they must also encourage members of the other religions, and those who do not wish to belong to any religion. The schools seek to develop thoughtful responsibility in pupils and, through religious education, to develop an

9

understanding of religions. The specific tasks of Christian nurture is thus heightened by the fact that the Church and the school can no longer be thought of as partners in Christian nurture.

23. There is another, perhaps still deeper, tension between educational ideals today and the task of Christian nurture. It is the tension between Christian faith as a tradition given to us from the past, and the educational ideal of the child-centred approach. The Churches of the west have for centuries been committed to an understanding of faith which saw it as intellectual agreement with given doctrines. In the early centuries of the Church, Christian experience was expressed in the creeds and in other documents which became the 'rule of faith'. The clergy, who could read these statements, told the beliefs to lay people, who gave their assent to them. So there arose a view of education in general, and Christian education in particular, which saw it as the passing on of intellectual knowledge.

24. But since the seventeenth and eighteenth centuries this view of the educational process has been severely criticised, largely on the grounds that it presents pre-digested knowledge in an inert form to the pupils. Worthwhile learning must be initiated and controlled by the learner, who must be actively involved in the learning. A great deal of the theological ferment of the last two centuries has similarly hinged upon the relationship between the givenness of the tradition and the reality of present-day experience. The divisions of the Western Church from the sixteenth century have reinforced the view that faith is commitment to doctrinal statements as standards of verbal correctness. Faith was further emphasized as being of an intellectual nature; this is indicated by the debates about whether infants, who could not understand, should be baptised.

25. So it is that the Church's commitment to this concept of received truth makes it difficult for Christians to come to terms with a view of education which emphasizes that the teacher must enable the child to express and formulate his own insights and ideas. Understood in this way, Christian faith is not open; it is a given, fixed and final truth, to which the believer makes no contribution but receives it in obedience. What then is the relationship between revelation and experience, and between education and evangelization? The evangelist seeks to summon the child to obedient response, but the educator encourages the child to respond to a wider range of material and ideas in a way only the pupil himself can discover. In this sense, education is open, but evangelism is not open. These are some of the puzzles which complicate the task of Christian nurture for the thoughtful Christian adult today.

4. CHANGES IN OUR UNDERSTANDING OF CHRISTIAN FAITH

26. The climate in which young people grow up into the Christian faith is deeply affected by how that faith is currently understood. We shall consider only those present day emphases which have a direct bearing on the processes of Christian nurture.

(a) In the sphere of *doctrine* the Churches have tended in recent years to be more tolerant and enquiring about the Christian faith; they have tended to see it less in terms of fixed doctrinal statements and more in terms of personal relations, and the investigation of various patterns of Christian meaning in life. Possibly the *Honest to God* debate, the death of God theology and the existential theology from the continent and America have contributed to this fluid and questioning approach to theology. Much theological discussion has centred around the peculiarity of religious language and the possibilities of giving a clear account of the logic and meaning of words used in religion. This has an obvious relevance to the tasks of Christian nurture, since the growing child must be helped to advance from simple to more complex understandings of the language of faith.

(b) Several generations of Christians have now learned to live with the idea that their knowledge of the *bible* is constantly developing in the light of new insights about ancient languages and cultures. This is still a thorny problem for large numbers of Christians. The line of conservative and liberal demarkation cuts right across denominations. Anxieties in this area reflect the failure of the Churches to take seriously their responsibility for theological education of their members. Insights from biblical theology and textual criticism should affect the way the bible is studied and the way it is taught to children. This is discussed in Chapter Five of this Report.

(c) The *Church* is thought of in a more unified way than it has been in recent decades, and there is a greater willingness to accept the positive implications of different denominational emphases. Lay people are being asked to accept more responsibility in the Churches, and the role of women in particular is expanding, but there is still little time given to adult education. There is also an increasing tendency to question accepted forms of ministry. Growing numbers of clergy are working in secular vocations. The mission of the Church is increasingly seen as being towards the service of humanity as a whole and not only in terms of self-propagation of Christianity through evangelism.

(d) In the sphere of *spirituality* there has been an upsurge of interest both inside and outside the Churches. Some young people are attracted to one of the mystical religions of the East; others seek an expansion of consciousness through the use of hallucinatory drugs, and, especially amongst older school pupils, there has been considerable interest in the occult.

This search for alternative ways of spiritual growth can be seen as a judgement on the Christian Churches, who have a rich variety of modes of

11

spirituality to offer. Certainly, there has been some increase in the provision of more varied and meaningful patterns of worship, but many of the more traditional Churches are finding that their young people are seeking religious sustenance from other sources.

Devotional practices, both in private and in families, have changed enormously since the early years of this century. Some Christians find a relevant form of spiritual life in social and political involvement rather than in traditional prayer and worship while others are being renewed by participation in the charismatic movement. In the Christian nurture of children it is important not to place before them one fixed form of Christian spirituality and devotional discipline, as if this were the sole authentic form of Christian life today.

(e) In the sphere of *ethics* Christian theology today tends to think less legalistically, less in terms of unchanging divine laws, and to respond more flexibly to situations many of which are being faced for the first time. Christian moral education cannot be as simple and as confident as it used to be.

(f) Finally, the fact that Christian faith is in dialogue with other world faiths, both religious and secular, has had an effect upon the climate of Christian nurture. Instead of seeking to supplant other faiths, more Christian are now prepared to listen, and to understand others. This is of particular importance for children and young people in the large cities, and in schools where the pluralism of our society is particularly evident.

Many of these theological trends are applied to the problems of Christian nurture in our fourth chapter.

27. The traditional patterns of Christian upbringing are no longer as effective as once they may have been, because the social, psychological, educational and theological climate in which nurture takes place is so very different. The kind of Christian nurture suitable for a culture dominated by a religious outlook is clearly not suitable for a culture dominated by a secular outlook. In this chapter of our Report, we have tried to describe some of the recent developments which are rendering traditional patterns of nurture obsolete. The remainder of this Report will explore the implications of these changes for how we should think of the task of Christian nurture today and will try to show some of the ways the Churches might respond positively to the new and critical situation now confronting them.

Chapter 3

A CHRISTIAN UNDERSTANDING OF CHILDHOOD

28. What do we as Christians believe about childhood? What significance does the Christian faith attach to children? If the Church's ministry to children is incoherent, it springs at least in part from our failure to ask such questions. Faith and practice are thus seldom integrated. When we do reflect about children in the Church, our anxiety is almost always to know what to do with them. The preoccupation with practical activities does not however mean that we approach our children without theological assumptions about them and their status. It may however often mean that we approach them with the wrong ones.

29. Our ideas about what it means to be a Christian relate mainly to adult models. Adults of almost every Christian tradition assume that belonging to the Church is a matter of believing certain things and doing certain things. But the things to believe are mostly things only adults can understand, the things to do are mostly things only adults can do. So these adult categories of faith and conduct do not provide a suitable theological framework for interpreting the place of the child in the church. Childhood requires a theology of its own. This does not mean that there is a different gospel for children, any more than there is a different gospel for women, it does mean that just as we seek to include in a predominantly masculine theology the feminine, so we must include childhood. (see para. 81). The task of a theology of childhood is to express a distinctively Christian understanding of the nature and status of childhood. Our concern here is not with what children are to believe and do about Christian faith, but how the Christian faith is to estimate the significance of the child. Too much of our theology has been concerned with an estimation of the adult, and especially the adult male.

30. Our concern is not with what Christians once believed about children and did to them, but rather with what, in the light of the whole Christian tradition, we believe about children today. In this, as in any theological discussion, the question of the authority behind what we affirm is fundamental. The use of the phrase 'the whole Christian tradition' is intended to remind us that what we believe about children (as about anything else) cannot be settled by appeal to the bible alone. We shall certainly examine the attitudes towards children found in the New Testament, but we shall not expect to find there a systematic Christian understanding of childhood. What we expect to find are events of theological significance, such as the dealings Jesus is reported to have had with children, and the childhood of Jesus himself. Our quest for a theology of childhood cannot stop with these events, but, especially in an ecumenical discussion, this is the right place to start.

JESUS AND THE CHILD

31. In studying the attitude of Jesus himself towards children our enquiries are impeded by two facts. First, the sayings about children in the gospels are related to each other in a very complicated way. The critical problems of disentangling them are considerable and too technical to discuss here. Second, these sayings have been sentimentalised in a deplorable manner. The sentiment of Christian romantic idealization of childhood lies like a layer of varnish over the words of Jesus. One of the tasks of the theologian is to try to dissolve this varnish.

32. We have one firm starting point. The words of Jesus about children are accompanied by actions. Jesus sets a child 'in the midst' of his disciples, then takes the child in his arms (Mk 9 33-37). Jesus takes children in his arms and blesses them (Mk. 10. 13-16). These are startling actions, without Old Testament precedent or rabbinic parallel. Thus even if the words of Jesus were from an early period taken to apply to 'little ones' in the sense of adult Christian disciples, their original reference was certainly to children themselves.

Jesus tells his disciples that true greatness lies in putting oneself last, at the service of all. The sign of this is the child set among them. Like one of the prophets, Jesus utters the word of God by what he does. The child, least significant in the community, placed in the centre of them, symbolises the only precedence Jesus recognises. Jesus identifies himself with the child.

'Whoever receives such child in my name receives me.' The acceptance of a child within the Church, and the service given to a child by the Church constitute an acknowledgement by the church of the Lordship of Christ. This may be understood mystically; it must be implemented practically. Christ is, as always, one with the most helpless (Mk. 9. 33-37,cf Matt.5 18. 1-5, Lk. 9. 46-48).

The disciples try to prevent children being brought to Jesus. The value of children in the Old Testament and in Judaism was their importance as 'the Israel to be'. In themselves they are not significant. Jesus, it is assumed, will share this attitude. His anger teaches otherwise. For it is to children and to those like them that the Kingdom of God belongs.

33. The word is spoken about each child and every child. The promise is boundless and unconditional. Historically, the Church has constantly sought to limit the promise of Jesus to a particular category of children, thus forbidding others and so repeating in every age the very sin which fired the anger of Jesus with his first disciples. The promise is not to innocent children, humble children, baptised, pious, or converted children. The promise is to children. The universality of the promise of the Kingdom to children constitutes a theological principle by which the Church in every age must guide its ministry to children, and a word of judgement on any policy towards children which would make discriminations and restrictions about *which* children it will accept and serve. If the Kingdom is already granted to

14

children, it is not because of any subjective qualities we may suppose them to possess, such as certain feelings or 'child-like' intuitions they may have. The Kingdom is theirs because objectively they are weak and helpless. The lowliness, that left to themselves they would die – these are their title-deeds to the highest place in the Kingdom of God.

The word of Jesus is that the reign of God is already exercised among children and the childlike. The child, like the adult who becomes a child, is a child of God. Thus he may utter the intimate 'Abba' of the Gethsemane prayer. Children say 'Abba' naturally. Adults must learn to say it or, better, never forget to say it. What unites the child and the childlike is that they are both dependent, a dependence not of servility but of trust (Mk. 10. 13-16, cf Mt 19. 13-15, Lk 18. 15-17).

INCARNATION AND CHRISTIAN GROWTH

34. When we look for a model of the growth of a child, we do not find it in the manufacture of an article in a factory. The product of a conveyor belt is un finished until the last part is fitted and the final screw is tightened. There is an important sense in which a human person, at any stage of his life, whether in maturity or old age, may be described as unfinished, in that there are unexplored possibilites of future growth and development still before him (see paragraph 57). But there is another sense in which the human being has a perfection proper to his stage of development whatever that stage may be, and in this sense, even a child, unlike a half-formed product of the conveyor belt, is truly finished. A child of three years old, or even three days old, is not defective because he cannot do what an adult can do. He is all that a three years old child or a three day old baby should be. The model for human growth must be a process which is perfect and complete in every stage and yet permits and demands further growth and change.

35. This model is provided for us by the concept of the incarnation. The Word became flesh and dwelt among us. But this is not something which happened to an adult. The early Church rejected the claim of the 'Adoptionists' that not until his baptism as an adult did the Eternal Word assume our human nature. When Christians speak of the incarnation they must first refer to the conception, the birth and the growing up of a child. Thus, traditional theology affirms that Jesus was neither more nor less the Son of God at the age of twenty or thirty than he was at the age of six months. The Word was incarnated fully and perfectly in the child as child, just as in the man as man. And yet the child grew.

36. This is the theological significance of the infancy narratives, notably of Luke. Luke tells us that Jesus grew in relationship with God and man (Lk 2. 40-52). His words echo the account of the boyhood of Samuel – again the varnish of sentiment has to dissolved – where the editor seems to have been at pains to stress that the child's physical growth was accompanied by a developing relationship with the Lord (1 Sam. 2.21, 26k; 3.19).

If there is theological purpose in Luke's words, it is to state that such a development was true of Jesus, that at every age of his childhood he is all that at that age a child should be. Throughout his childhood Jesus enjoys that completeness of life in relation to God proper to his age which is the expression in childhood of his perfect humanity. He achieved manhood through temptation and struggle, just as he achieved childhood through passing through the earlier stages of growth and learning. But, if we take the model of the incarnation seriously, his status as divine Son of God remains absolute at every stage. Being Son of God is not the achievement of Jesus, but the gift of the eternal will of God (see paragraph 55). So in this model, we have that mixture of finished perfection allied with continuous growth which we need to understand childhood in a Christian way.

37. Jesus is the normal child in the sense that his childhood is normative. There is a pattern of human childhood in the childhood of Jesus. The essence of this pattern is not that 'Christian children all must be, mild, obedient, good as he'. The child Jesus does not tell today's children how to behave. But the childhood of Jesus does confer on human childhood infinite worth. If the humanity of Jesus was as perfectly expressed by his childhood as by his manhood, then it must be affirmed that there is potentially for every child, at every age, an appropriate Christian maturity. Whether at ten years, ten months, or ten days there is the right relationship to God fitted to that age.

38. In the light of the Incarnation, childhood can no longer be regarded as merely a provisional and a preparatory episode. The childhood of Jesus does not allow the Church any understanding of childhood that measures the child by what, not yet being an adult, he lacks. Jesus was a child. This forbids our beginning exclusively with some definition of what a Christian should be in terms of what a Christian *adult* should be and then planning only *what* must be done to turn the child into the man. Our theology of childhood concentrates on the 'continuous now' of the child's life, just as we emphasize the 'now' of the adult's life, without neglecting what the child and the adult will someday become. A child at any age may be wholly human and wholly God's. Because Christ was a child, a child can be a Christian.

THE CHILD IN THE CHURCH

39. It is important to ask what is the child's status in the Church, but it is more important to ask what, for the child, *is* the Church. Some would answer that for the child his family is the church and would suggest that the New Testament phrase 'the church in his house' (Rom. 16:5 etc.) is indicative of such an understanding from early Church times, assuming that, once the head of the house had become a Christian, the whole household, chlildren included, would have been baptised and thereafter constitute a church.

Many would refute this equation, contending not only the biblical exegesis but also the lack of realistic appraisal of the contemporary situation in child-family-church relationships. Certainly research findings of psychiatrists, such as Dr. R.D. Laing, would indicate the complexities in family relationships and would not encourage a safe basis for the simple equation of church — family for all children.

The fact remains that despite or in spite of family circumstances, lack of a nuturing Christian community, experience supposedly to the contrary, the grace of God can be known in childhood as inexplicably and mysteriously as at other times.

40. For the fortunate children, however, from caring homes, whether their parents be Christian or not, it is true that in early childhood the grace of God can be known mainly through the mediation of parents. In Judaism it was understood that the child's life with his parents contained, indeed constituted, his life in the Lord. In Christ, the family relationship is charged with a new quality and character.The parent-child relationship is, in the Pauline terms, 'in the Lord'. The exchange between child and parent is no longer fundamentally obedience for command but trust for love. But it is still within the personal relationships of family life that a child's relationship to God is to grow (Eph. 6 1-4, cf 3. 14-15).

41. Within the New Testament period, the right of the child to belong to the Church was never called in question. The child belongs to his family and, if his family belongs to the Church, so does he. If this is nowhere stated as a principle, it is because it nowhere arises as a matter of controversy. If in our own time the status of the child in the Church is disputed, then this first and fundamental principle must be explicitly affirmed. The child belongs to the Church. The Church is a necessary agent in his nurture, giving a wider context and greater stimulus than that provided by his family. His upbringing as a Christian is nurture within the family of God, not the evangelism of one outside it.

42. What of the child whose family renounces any allegiance to the Church? In earliest childhood the love of God can still be known only through his parents or those adults in whose care he is. His home can still be his Church and should be recognised as such by the wider Church. Moreover the Lord of the Church has said that the Kingdom of God belongs to this child. The Kingdom is bigger than the Church. There will be many such children (and many who are childlike) to whom the Kingdom belongs who are not formally admitted to the church. In receiving such within its fellowship, the Church does not make them children of God but affirms joyfully what they already see (see paragraph 119).

43. Children are a gift to the Church. The Lord of the Church sets them in the midst of the Church, today as in Galilee, not as objects of benevolence, nor even as recipients of instruction, but in the last analysis as patterns of discipleship. The Church that does not accept children unconditionally in to its fellowship is depriving those children of what is rightfully theirs, but the deprivation such as Church will itself suffer is far more grave.

Jesus helps the fishermen - Lisa Faulkner 5 yrs

Chapter 4

AN UNDERSTANDING OF CHRISTIAN NURTURE

44. The Christian life is one of continual growth. 'Go on growing in the grace and in the knowledge of our Lord and Saviour Jesus Christ' (2 Peter 3.18). The Christian has 'put on a new self which will progress towards true knowledge the more it is renewed in the image of its creator' (Col. 3.10). The demand for constant development in Christian character and insight extends to children, for parents, 'in bringing them up (are to) correct them and guide them as the Lord does' (Eph 6.4). It includes adults, who, when they become Christians, are to be hungry for the milk which will help them to grow up to salvation (1 Peter 2.2), and it applies even to the greatest Christian leaders and saints. Paul writes, 'I have not become perfect yet; I have not yet won, but I am still running, trying to capture the prize for which Christ Jesus captured me' (Phil 3.12).

45. Christian nurture is one of the terms used to describe everything which aids this process of growth. It may include study of the bible (2 Tim 3.14-17), the ministry of preachers and teachers (1 Cor 3.5f), and the mutual criticism and appeals of the Christian congregation (1 Cor 14.26). Paul is particularly fond of describing the Christian life as a 'walking' (Eph. 4.1 Rom. 8.4) and in Acts the Christian life is described as the 'way' (Acts 9.2). Nurture is everything which helps Christians to walk that way.

46. We understand Christian nurture first of all when we see that it springs out of the nature of the Christian life itself as a process of continuous growth. This growth does not take place in isolation, but in company with others who are also walking in the same way. Our understanding of nurture is thus bound up with our understanding of the church, the community of the way.

PARENTS AND CHRISTIAN NURTURE

47. We are mainly concerned with the *Christian* nurture of children. We are concerned not primarily with the kind of general nurture into loving community which all children need, whether they be from Christian families or not, but with that understanding of specifically Christian nurture which grows out of the New Testament and out of the nature of the Church. Just as it is perfectly proper to speak of the nurture of the children of Muslim families into the full life of Islam, and similarly, the nurture of Humanist children into the values and ideals of Humanism, so we are concerned to describe a nurture which is distinctively Christian. Indeed, one of the reasons why, for many Christian parents, the whole idea of nurture has become difficult is precisely because Christian nurture must become more self-conscious and more specific in a society in which different religious and non-religious

traditions exist side by side in mutual respect. The parent committed to one of these traditions cannot leave the responsibility of nurture into the things most deeply cherished by his tradition to society as a whole. He, with his community, must take deliberate steps to promote the nurture of the young of his faith. This involves the conscious selection of Christian faith, as one amongst many possible faiths, as the context and goal of this specific nurture. It is this very deliberation, this choice of one way and the consequent rejection (loving and tolerant though it be) of other ways, which presents problems for the thoughtful Christian living in a pluralistic society. 'What right have parents to decide their children's commitment?' we ask ourselves. Should children not be encouraged 'to make up their own minds?' 'How can we presume that our own choice of the Christian faith is a choice other people should make, even our own children?' These difficulties arise out of Christian nurture, considered as a *deliberate* activity, carried out towards *children* who are necessarily easily influenced, in a society in which Christian faith is but *one alternative* amongst many.

48. Clearly, it is impossible *not* to influence children. Those parents who believe that 'you should never influence a child about religion one way or the other' will not be able to put their belief into practice, for the simple reason that, if they are practising Christians, their children are bound to know it. Sooner or later, their children will know that not all parents go to church, not all pray, not all possess a loved and used copy of the bible. Parents who are Christians are inevitably creating an environment within which something of Christian faith will be acquired. Nurture of this sort may not be conscious on the part of the parents, but as soon as reflection takes place, then nurture must be either abandoned (which means abandoning the Christian presence in the home and abandoning the child to other influences) or become deliberate. Since it is impossible not to influence a child, it cannot be wrong in itself to influence him; on the contrary, it must be a duty of parenthood to attempt to influence the child properly. The inescapable responsibility to nurture lies in the nature of the parent-child relationship. The child lives, for his first few years, within the psychological, social, political and religious world of his parents. The proper ordering of these influences is as much a part of parenthood as the providing of food and shelter. Therefore the ethical problems of Christian nurture do not arise from the question whether to nurture or not, but in deciding what the proper functions and limits of Christian nurture should be.

CHRISTIAN NURTURE: EDUCATION, INSTRUCTION AND INDOCTRINATION

49. The functions and limits of Christian nurture in a modern, open, democratic society can best be considered by contrasting Christian nurture with other processes, such as indoctrination, instruction and secular education.

50. In recent years, secular education has been thought of as an open, critical, person-centred process of learning which opens up possibilities of further learning. Education is concerned with learning worthwhile things in worthwhile ways, and it promotes an attitude of continuous enquiry. It is not neutral, in so far as education has to decide what things really *are* worthwhile, but it is neutral in the sense that it is continuously critical about itself, and instead of simply telling children these worthwhile things, it seeks to build up their independence, their autonomy as persons. It is a worthwhile thing in itself to be a thoughtful person, thinking things out for oneself, and not simply taking things on the authority of what other people say. In so far as Christians, Humanists, Muslims and Communists can all be free, thoughtful, enquiring people, secular education can *result in* all these varieties of commitment, but it cannot, in our western world, seek *only* to make Christians, or *only* to make Humanists. If that were the case, then only children of the favoured community could attend the state schools; others would have to have schools of their own, or each community of faith would have to have its own schools. It is easy to see that if we want to have schools in which mutual respect and common understanding will be fostered for life in an open society, then state education must rest on values common to democracy. Otherwise, we could have nothing but sectarian systems of schools, not a common system of schools for all the children.

51. But Christian nurture seeks only to deepen Christian faith and life. We must therefore distinguish between the secular education of an open society and the Christian nurture of a part of that open society. Certainly we may speak of a Christian understanding of this secular education, in the sense that Christian faith may actually lead to the creation of such secular education in a society such as ours, but this understanding of secular education will still differ from Christian nurture carried out by the Churches, for the latter seeks only to deepen Christian enquiry, while education seeks for further general enquiry and personal development whether leading to Christian faith or not.

52. Instruction is a content-centred, authoritative 'telling' which passes on previously acquired knowledge and skills. The instructor knows the facts, he knows the truth, and he finishes his instruction when pupils have learned from him the facts and skills and truths which he conveys to them. Instruction may be to do with learning the skills which will get you a job; secular education is to do with becoming a reflective person; Christian nurture is to do with becoming a Christian person.

53. Indoctrination, however, seeks to deprive a person of his personhood by securing more conformity to a set of doctrines, a conformity which will not be swayed by evidence or rational argument, a wearing down of the will and the imagination by constant repetition and by deliberately avoiding discussion of alternatives.

Let us have a closer look at the differences between Christian nurture and secular education inspired by Christian ideals.

54. Personhood may be thought of as both a gift and an achievement (see

21

paragraph 36). It is a *gift* in so far as a child is made a person by his interaction with his parents and other persons. He is given life, speech conscience, awareness of sexual identity, and so on, along with the circumstances of his birth – his nationality, his father's or mother's occupation, the locality in which they live. Personhood is an *achievement* in so far as a person is created by his own free decisions won against sufferings and disadvantages.

55. Not to nurture a child in the tradition of his family is to deny him that part of his self-hood which should be given to him. It is to deny him the past, which is his own past, out of which his creation of his own unique selfhood should take place. But if a child is nurtured so as to give him not only his past but his future as well, to determine his future beyond his own power of changing it or creating it, then that part of his personhood which should be his own achievement is denied him. This is one of the most important principles of a truly Christian nurture – to give the past but not to close the future.

56. This view of man, which looks upon him as being unfinished (see paragraph 34), is a central feature of the Christian view of man. 'We are already the children of God,' writes John, 'but what we are to be in the future has not yet been revealed' (1 John 3.2). Previous generations of the faithful are also incomplete, so the author of the letter to the Hebrews writes, since they are 'not to reach perfection except with us' (Heb 11.40). Paul says, 'The knowledge that I have now is imperfect; but then I shall know as fully as I am known' (1 Cor 13.12). It is because of the unfinished state of our humanity that the Christian life is one of constant growth, and the Christian life is described as 'the way'.

57. Secular education and Christian nurture have this in common: they both seek to give the child his past so as to enable him to create his own future. But whereas education conceives of this future broadly in terms of the values of our liberal democracy, Christian nurture conceives of it in terms of the Christian future. Secular education fails if a person becomes a bigot but not if he becomes an atheist. Christian nurture fails *both* if he becomes a bigot *and* if he becomes an atheist. Certain things about the future have been decided in Christian faith, since Christ is both Alpha and Omega, first and last. Christian nurture is thus less open towards the future than secular education, and it is more specific in its intentions, namely, to create a Christian future. Christian nurture occupies a middle position between closed and authoritative instruction on the one hand, in which the past is simply reduplicated, and open, enquiring education on the other.

FAITH, LIFE AND HISTORY IN THE NURTURE PROCESS

58. But how can nurture be distinguished from indoctrination, which deprives a child of his independence altogether? For Christian nurture seeks to create a *Christian* future. Is this not to determine the future of the child? Any nurturing group which seeks to work in the middle of a plural society in which

an open, critical kind of education is functioning will be exposed to the charge that it is indoctrinatory, simply because it selects one possible future (in the case of Christian nurture, a Christian future) and ignores others. But there is nothing particularly praiseworthy about being completely open towards the future. Even secular education is not completely open in this way, since education fails if it produces bigots; there are certain outcomes which would not be compatible with the ideals of education. Only nihilism, or anarchism, a denial of all continuity and a refusal to be committed to any values, would be completely open towards the future. In Christian nurture, the past is not cancelled out, nor is it used as a strait-jacket. It is a springboard, or a launching-pad, or a womb.

59. What does it mean to seek to create the Christian future? A religion can only encourage the personal freedom of its young people towards their future if the religion is free with regard to its own future. If Christian faith sought merely to reduplicate itself, to form young Christians who were the exact repetition of the previous generation, to pass on Christian faith as if it were like a parcel handed down from generation to generation, then it would be very difficult to distinguish between the passing on of this sort of thing and closed, authoritative instruction or even indoctrination.

60. But the Christian faith is such that it can only be passed on if it is renewed in the reception (see paragraph 73). Christian faith is constantly critical of itself. Christianity itself is in process of changing, and it always has been. There is no fixed and final form of Christian faith, and this is why there can be no fixed and final form of nurture into it. 'When the Spirit of Truth comes, he will lead you to the complete truth' (John 16.13). In 2 Corinthians 3.7 and 18 Paul describes the growth of Christian faith from glory to glory, constantly transcending its previous level, concluding 'We with our unveiled faces reflecting like mirrors the brightness of the Lord, all grow brighter and brighter as we are turned into the image that we reflect. This is the work of the Lord who is Spirit.'

61. The continual growth and development of the Christian faith is based on the fact that the central focus of God's revelation is not in a book, a document, but in a person, who himself 'increased in wisdom, in stature, and in favour with God and men' (Luke 2.52). Christian teaching does not simply teach about the Jesus of the past, as if he was finally and fully known by the past. This would be to 'know Christ in the flesh' (2 Cor. 5.16). What the church confesses is a Christ who is still being formed in us (Gal 4.19). So, if Christ is taught as if the past fully contained him, we would have instruction, the passing on, in a way which is finished and complete, of previously acquired, unchanging knowledge. The past is then nothing but the past. But Christ was transfigured, resurrected, and he continues to appear to his Church as the one 'who is, who was and who is to come' (Rev. 1.8). Can we, for example, instruct children in the meaning of Christmas, as if that meaning were wholly given to us in its completeness from the past? That would be to lock Christmas up in the past, to make it a celebration of past time, instead of the celebration of the breaking into time of eternity. But the meaning of Christmas is still being

unfolded. We and our children will contribute to it.

62. What is it, then, to seek to create a Christian future for our children? It cannot be to deny them their own distinctive contribution to it, or to close the future for them, or to seek to make little copies of ourselves. This would no longer be Christian nurture, because it would not be true to the developing nature of Christian faith. It would instead be to offer religious instruction about Christianity, or, if it tried to produce an irrational commitment, it might even become indoctrination. It is because Christian faith is like it is that it can offer a nurture which both puts the child into dialogue with his past, and also leaves him free to develop his own personhood, in continuity with that past, but in a manner which we, the nurturers, cannot predict. This is also the reason why Christian faith is able to understand and even to produce a view of secular education which sets education free for constant scrutiny and further enquiry.

63. This means that when Christians seek to nurture their young into Christian faith, they literally do not fully know what they are nurturing them into. They only know what they are nurturing them out of, i.e. out of the Christian past. They know the resources but not the use which will be made of them. What we pass on to our children is not the painting but the paintbox.

64. The young, it is often said, are the future of the Church. The future of Christian community is not so unrestricted, not so broad and general towards its future as secular education is, but on the other hand, it is not so closed about its future as to permit instruction or indoctrination.

FAITH AND THE NURTURING COMMUNITY

65. There is, then, one sense in which the Christian future is known ('we shall be like him' 1 John 3.2) and another sense in which it remains as yet unknown ('What we are to be in the future has not yet been revealed'). This can be described as a sort of faithful uncertainty. It is not the uncertainty of the gambler who never knows which way the chips will fall. Christians know that God will bring 'everything together under Christ, as head' (Eph. 1.10). It is not the uncertainty of disbelief, but the certainty of Abraham who 'set out without knowing where he was going' (Heb. 11.8). The task of Christian nurture is to develop a future in which the uncertainty of doubt is replaced by the uncertainty of faith.

66. This tension between the known and the unknown can be further considered in the light of the relationships between the generations in the Church. This will also help to show how the nature of Christian nurture springs out of the nature of the Church itself. Although nurture is mainly directed towards the young, we have seen already that the adult is also to be nurtured. Pastoral care is offered to the sick and the dying, but nurture is offered to the normal and healthy of whatever age, who are still learning and growing. The nurturing task of the Church is thus one and indivisible. The children of Abraham learn to journey as they wander with faithful Abraham. Abraham

tells them where he has been. That is their most common past. But now they travel on together. That is their future. Together, the generations offer each other a mutual nurture. The idea of a community in transit which is found in the speech of Stephen in Acts 7, and in Hebrews 11, is basic for an understanding of Christian nurture. The Church lives not only because adult passes on experiences to child, but because both adult and child share new experiences, which are interpreted in the light of the tradition. The tradition itself is renewed in the process.

67. So Abraham learns with Isaac and even from Isaac. Isaac unwittingly asks his father a question which pushes Abraham into a new insight. 'Where is the lamb for the burnt offering?' (Gen. 22.7). This does not involve any denial of the responsibility or the expertise of the adult. But it does mean that the nature of Christian nurture is determined by the child as well as by the adult. The adult symbolises one aspect of the tradition. It is old and has already travelled far. The child symbolises an equally valid aspect of the tradition. It is always youthful, growing and being renewed. So we read that the adult if he would enter into the kingdom of God, must 'be born again' (John 3.3f) and become 'like a little child' (Mark 10.15) but the child must become 'fully mature with the fullness of Christ himself. Then we shall not be children any longer' (Eph. 4.13f). The child and the adult constantly change place in the symbolism of Christian nurture. The image of the child Samuel awakening from sleep to receive the message of the Lord to his people to the congregation. These are the 'parts' of Christian nurture. The hope of Christian nurture is that when the perfect comes, the partial shall disappear. Only the divine love offers the church this final unity. Then there will be no more 'knowing myself as a child' or 'knowing myself as an adult' but 'I shall know as fully as I am known' (1 Cor. 13.11f).

THE TASK OF THE NURTURING COMMUNITY

68. The task of Christian nurture must be seen not only in domestic terms, as something taking place within the families and generations of the Church, but also within the larger context of the Church's universal mission to humanity. The mission of the Church is God's mission. It is the initiative of God towards mankind. The task of the Church is to discover and respond to the mission of God. The Church is certainly not the only agency of divine mission; nor are the present, visible, Christian communities the goal of the mission. The image of the Church as the body of Christ could be misleading, because it might suggest that the only access of God through Christ to the world is through the visible Christian Churches. The task of the Church would then be seen as multiplying itself and so 'spreading' the incarnation. But then Christian nurture could easily be thought of as being nothing but religious socialization, inducting the young into the life of the institutionalised churches. Christian nurture should however enable young people (and their elders) to recognise the mission of God wherever He may be active in our world, and

to participate in it. It is even possible that thorough socialization into the life of a local church, with perhaps limited horizons and merely parochial interests, might actually hinder young people in responding to God's universal mission. (See para. 106f).

69. We see then that although we cannot understand the meaning of Christian nurture without understanding the Church, the Church itself can only be understood not in relation to Christ alone, nor God the Father only, but as in relation to Christ a line, nor to God as Father only, but it flows out of the nature of God as Father, Son and Holy Spirit, one name. Into this one name Christians are baptised (Mat 28.19). Christian nurture helps us to take baptism seriously, as drawing us into the loving will of the Triune God for all people.

Chapter 5

THE BIBLE IN CHRISTIAN NURTURE

70. Christian nurture may be looked on as a process of initiation, initiation into a tradition; or for those who do not like the word 'tradition', initiation into a way. This process of nurturing or initiating people also means involving them in a community, the community of faith. To nurture each other in this community means to help or enable each other to live in a Christian way.

71. To nurture each other means communicating to each other certain things. Three main areas of communication may be considered. They are mentioned here not in order of importance.

(a) WORKING KNOWLEDGE

Christian nurture does involve communicating a body of knowledge. Christians, to be Christians at all, need to know certain things about Jesus, for example. They need to know what have traditionally been regarded as the facts about his life, death and resurrection, and a good deal about his teaching. They need to know what Christians have traditionally believed – the contents of the creeds, broadly speaking. It is useful for them to know that the Christian community traces its parentage to old Israel, and to know something about the 'mighty acts' of salvation on which the people of God founded their faith. If they are to play an active part in the Church's life they will eventually need to know something about the structure of their church and how the organization 'works'. They need to be instructed (the word is appropriate here) about such basic matters as how to find their way around the bible and what to do at holy communion.

To communicate such things is not to provide people with faith, but merely to give them a working knowledge of the ways in which it is conventionally expressed.

(b) A WAY OF DOING THINGS

Nurture involves communicating a way of doing things. This can only happen in community (in a family or in the church) and it happens less by instruction than by imitation. This 'way of doing things' involves both the way Christians do things *together* (i.e. inside the family and inside the church) and also how they behave and what they do in the world at large. The way of doing things varies a good deal from one Christian community to another, but there is nevertheless something which can be identified as a common Christian way.

(c) A WAY OF LOOKING AT THINGS

Nurture involves communicating a way of looking at things. This is bound up with the working knowledge which was talked about in paragraph (a), for the tradition provides plenty of guidance about how Christians generally have looked at things. It is also bound up with the 'way of doing things' in paragraph (b), because the way Christians go about things depends directly on Christian attitudes and values.

So all these three, the 'working knowledge', the 'way of doing things' and the 'way of looking at things' are interdependent, and together they add up to a way of living.

72. We grow into the tradition, the way, and the tradition guides as well as assist our growth. But it does not impose uniformity on us. It acknowledges 'varieties of gifts, but the same Spirit... varieties of service, but the same Lord' (1 Cor. 12.4). Our growth is growth in freedom, freedom to be ourselves. It is a growth towards maturity, and a growth in maturity; a maturity 'measured by nothing less than the full stature of Christ' (Eph. 4.13). Christian nurture is therefore very different from the inculcation of a fixed set of beliefs and a fixed set of rules of conduct (which is an idea one might easily get from looking at some older catechisms).

73. The Christian way is not something fixed and unchanging. A living way is not a way that never changes, but one which remains true to itself. The mark of a living tradition is not immutability but continuity. Christian growth is thus not a matter of simply taking over the tradition, or of swallowing what it offers us, but rather of *responding* to what is offered. As we grasp it, make it our own, it does something to us. But at the same time *we* do something to *it*, as we interpret it to meet our own needs, and as we put to it the questions which face us now. We become new people by walking in the Christian way, but the way it self is continually renewed by those who walk in it. (see paragraph 60).

THE BIBLE AND CHRISTIAN NURTURE

74. The bible is basic. Christian nurture cannot ignore it, and indeed, many of the resources of nurture come directly or indirectly from it. It is only from the bible that we know anything about the events of our Lord's life and death and resurrection, or about the coming of the Holy Spirit to his first followers. It is one of the main sources of knowledge (and for the early period our only source of knowledge) about the past of the community of believers. It is the bible, therefore, which enables us to discover both our own past and God's ancient, saving acts.

75. But the bible does not give us bare information. It gives us access to the *experience* of believers of other generations. To make the fullest use of the bible in Christian nurture we must first examine that initial experience, as far as the scriptures allow us to do so; we should try to see how it has been understood by subsequent generations, and finally relate it to our own experience of God in our own age and place. We thus broaden and deepen our own experiences by entering into that of prophets, apostles and saints.

Unless we share a little of that experience before we begin, we shall not understand what the bible is talking about. But unless we share more of it by the time we finish, then no nurturing will actually have taken place. The bible interacts with our existing experience, deeper experience leading to profounder understanding of the bible, and profounder understanding of the bible leading to a deepening of experience.

76. This interaction, and this contribution from our own experience, is necessary if the bible is genuinely to speak to us now. By itself the bible speaks only of the past. It has to be looked at in the light of our own experience and related to that experience before it speaks to the present at all. It does not by itself answer the question: What is the way of faith today? and we cannot answer this question merely by repeating biblical phrases and statements. The bible provides the starting point for an answer. It helps to control the answer, for certain answers can be shown to be clearly incompatible with it. But to use the bible as if it were self-sufficient, and as if it *prescribed* particular ways of Christian living, would be to instruct or even indoctrinate, not to nurture.

77. The bible, when used in Christian nurture, is bound to be used selectively. Christians have never, in fact, used the bible as if all parts of it were of equal weight and value. Jesus himself used the bible selectively, allowing certain parts of it to control the interpretation of others. We must acknowledge that some parts are more relevant and vital than others to our present experience; some parts speak more readily to us than others.

78. The necessity to use the bible selectively raises acute problems. Doubtless there would be a large measure of agreement among Christians as to the centrality of some passages, but there might be a considerable measure of disagreement about others. We need to be careful lest we leave aside some passages for the wrong reasons. We may be tempted to neglect them not because they do not speak to us but because they speak too challengingly.

79. The problems of selectivity, acute as they are, become even more serious when it is the nurture specifically of children that is in question. There is probably little to be gained by introducing children to passages of the bible which they cannot relate to their own experience, even though they may enjoy them as stories. On the other hand, if we allow our selection to be dictated purely by what the child is able to appreciate we may end up with a selection which is unrepresentative of the bible as a whole. The important thing is that the diet on which we nurture our children should fairly represent the bible's message, though this message need not always be conveyed by using the bible's own words or even its imagery. The truths which the nurturer perceives in the bible may need to be translated into non-bliblical language and conveyed in stories or activities relating closely to the child's own experience and interests.

80. As an illustration, we may briefly consider the parables of Jesus. In the parables Jesus attempts to convey truth by using metaphors or pictures which

his audience understood and with which they were thoroughly familiar. They knew without being told the method by which the Palestinian peasant sowed his seed, and the reason for it. To them these images had a compelling logic of their own. The modern reader of a parable is often in the position of a man who has to have a joke explained to him. The image which was meant to clarify has become for him something to be clarified. To remain true to the bible and its method the nurturer ought often to abandon the bible's own image or story and find an alternative which is *immediately* understood and which makes its own point without the necessity of explanation. It goes without saying that this puts a heavy responsibility on the nurturer to make sure that he, at least, thoroughly understands the original and what it means.

81. The gospel which we present to our children must not be a different gospel from that which we deem appropriate to adults. Neither must our exegesis of the bible be a different one. Though we must adapt our expression of it to the experience and understanding of the child, the content of what is expressed must remain the same. (see paragraph 29).

82. If we continue to present the bible to children we ought to examine carefully our motives for doing so. Bible teaching is often given, not because it really helps the child's understanding, but because it makes the teacher feel better. The teacher tells a bible story, and tells it well, and feels a great sense of satisfaction, a conviction that something must have been achieved. This is to assume that bible teaching is somehow self-justifying, an end in itself. But the aim of presenting biblical material is to increase Christian understanding. Where understanding can be more readily promoted by other means, we must cheerfully adopt them.

83. This is not to over look the educational value of the story, as such. Stories relating to the child's own experience can be very valuable. But the story is not to be used as a *substitute* for the child's own experience, and this is how bible stories are frequently used.

THE BIBLE AND CRITICISM

84. The interpretation of the bible cannot remain the same from age to age because the Christian community and its ways of looking at and thinking about the world do not stand still. Moreover, our knowledge of the bible itself, of the background against which it was produced and the process by which it took shape has increased at an explosive rate over the last one hundred and fifty years.

85. This does not mean that we should teach biblical and historical criticism to young children, but that we should not present the bible to children as if criticism did not exist. We ought not to present biblical material in such a way as to make it hard for the child to relate his biblical knowledge to other areas of knowledge. We ought not to present the bible in such away that he cannot relate the world of the bible to the world of which he learns in the physics or biology or geography lesson at school.

86. For example: it would be improper, and in the long run perhaps not very fruitful, to deal with the doctrine of creation simply by expounding Genesis 1-2. A twentieth-century Christian who only understands the doctrine of creation in terms of what is said in the book of Genesis has an inadequate and defective understanding of the subject. The child has not begun to understand what the bible says about creation until he has related what the bible says to what he has learnt in biology about evolution and what his encyclopaedias say about the probable origins of the solar system. Indeed, in practice it is probably better to begin with the biology, physics, geography and astronomy, and *then* ask, How does the bible suggest we look at this knowledge?

87. For the nurturer himself a critical and historical understanding of the bible is not an optional extra, or something which he can leave to the experts. Without some historical and background knowledge we can easily mislead ourselves, e.g. by quoting biblical sayings regardless of the situation which produced them; a situation which may be very different from the one to which we are trying to apply them. Whatever may be said of the nurtured, therefore, the nurturer himself ought to be familiar with critical approaches to the bible and have come to terms with them.

THE ROLES OF CHURCH AND SCHOOL IN EXPLORING THE BIBLE

88. The differing roles of school and Church, and perhaps of the family (see paragraph 113), in presenting the bible to children, need to be carefully defined. Quite different ways of approaching the bible are appropriate respectively, to Church and school. (The church school may present special problems.) In the Christian community, the bible is presented by people who avowedly accept its insight, and are known to do so by those who entrust children to them. They therefore present it in a committed way. They are not only entitled to do this but their ministry obliges them to do so. That is what they are there for. This commitment is one of the things implied by describing what they do as 'Christian nurture'. In the secular schools, what is going on is not the nurture of Christians, but the education of young people for a pluralist society, and the bible therefore *ought not*, in that context, to be presented from a position of Christian commitment. This is not to say that religious education in secular schools cannot be done by committed Christian people, but that in doing it they will be conscious that they are doing a different job, in a different way from when, for example, they assist in a Sunday school or conduct worship in church.

THE BIBLE AND WORSHIP

89. The point about selectivity needs to be made again here. There are

very few passages from the bible which can appropriately be read in worship to children (and perhaps adults) without some introduction or explanation, albeit brief. Such is the gap between the modern world and the bible that to read the bible in public without comment is at best a solemn waste of time and at worst an exercise in misleading the faithful.

Traditional church lessons are almost always too long; the use of modern versions is to be generally encouraged. It goes without saying that any scripture reading, to be effective, must be a genuine part of the act of worship, related to the other parts, and that somewhere in the service it ought to be expounded or its relevance to the theme or subject explicitly pointed out. Methods of presenting scriptural material other than by straight reading are worth exploring.

Chapter 6

CHRISTIAN NURTURE AND RESPONSE
INDIVIDUAL AND CORPORATE

90. We have seen that the needs of an individual cannot be understood in isolation from others, for a person exists in a network of relationships. In the bible, the human personality is not divided into the various components of body (flesh), mind and spirit. Man is understood in terms of the wholeness of personality for which in the New Testament the word 'body' is used. When St. Paul exhorted the Roman 'to present their bodies as a living sacrifice', he meant 'present yourselves' (Rom. 12.1). The argument in 1 Corinthians 12 on the 'oneness' of the body and its various organs, as an analogy of the church, suggests that whatever part of the natural body is envisaged, it has to do with the integrity of the whole self. The diversity of gifts in the church points to the unity of the Spirit.

91. From the biblical standpoint, to be a person is to be in relationship, and this relatedness is between persons and with God. The central concern in the bible is with the formation of persons and therefore the making of a community. Individuals are called into community and personal growth takes place within community. Community does not obliterate individuals. On the contrary, it is a necessary context for individual life, and whatever tensions there are between the individual and the community, they are not set over against each other but belong together.

AIMS OF CHRISTIAN NURTURE

92. If we wish to measure our success and failure in the Christian nurture of our children we must be clear about our aims and objectives. As we have already briefly noticed, sociologists and psychologists can help us enormously in our understanding of how attitudes are shaped and the stages of development through which children pass in the process of learning (paragraphs 17-19). Our understanding of children now is such that we have no excuse for seeing them merely as the recipients of tradition or only as adults in the making. Nurture must mean taking seriously each stage of children's growth. It must be 'child-related' in the sense that techniques of nurture, in order to be effective, must take into account our ever-increasing knowledge of child development. The child must always be taken seriously *now*. Religious nurture must begin with a religious understanding of *him*.

93. Psychological research, however, cannot tell us what should be the aim of Christian nurture. For this we must go to the New Testament and Christian tradition, and here we learn that it is about the building up of a

person into the life of Christ, which involves an integration of the individual into the life of a Christian community and a building up of the whole church into the fullness of Christ. It is a life-long process with many critical moments. In some traditions it is the process initiated by baptism, while in others it is a process which leads up to baptism. It presupposes a living community as a necessary context, for that is the nature of Christian life, and without it there can be no real individual growth. Individual commitment will be to the Person of Christ as he is made known to the individual believer within the life of the Christian community. Individual belief is making the belief of the church one's own.

CHRISTIAN INITIATION

94. The quality of human relationships experienced by the child within the Christian community will therefore have a crucial influence on his religious development, and the sad truth is that many Christian communities are not concerned for the quality of their life as a context for nurture. They are, of course, anxious for the children's growth in faith, but they do not appear to appreciate that the nature and quality of their life together, and the children's involvement in it, are critical for development.

95. If we look carefully at our approach to children and the technqiues we use in dealing with them in the Church, we shall find that they have been moulded by educational practices of the last century. The dominant view then was that children must be prepared for their roles in society, which, for the independent school was that of leadership, and for the rest was to accept one's station in life and learn how to be subordinate. Both were concerned with an eventual social role, and the needs of children at any given age were subordinated to the needs of a future adult role. This inductive view moulded our practices within the Church. Our failure to understand and provide for the needs of children is largely responsible for the breakdown of nurture. This is why our rethinking of Christian nurture must begin with a Christian understanding of children.

96. The integration of children into the Christian community is therefore essential. Is it not significant that when we talk of dealing with our children we use words which suggest they stand over against the community rather than being members of it? We speak of 'training' them, 'educating' them, 'instructing' them. We rarely talk of 'ministering' to them or of a 'ministry to children' as a section of the community, as we speak of a ministry to the elderly or to the sick. This point is made in a contribution from the Orthodox tradition.

The whole attitude of Christian society to the child is fundamentally different in Orthodox and Western spheres. A child of Orthodox parents will be brought up in the Church whereas in the West the child will be trained by the Church, his parents, and possibly his school, to bring him to a point of readiness necessary before the Church can accept him as a full member. This distinction is linked with the fact that in the Orthodox Church, the

34

Sacraments of Baptism, Confirmation and First Communion are given to the child at the age of a few weeks or months, and therefore the child is fully eligible to be brought up *in* the Church. In the West, although Infant Baptism is generally the rule, Confirmation follows at a later age, and is preceded by a period of moral and intellectual instruction by the Church... The child of Orthodox parents has a recognised status in the Church from birth. He is never looked on either as a sinful little alien to be saved or something preciously individual to be left to his own conscience. The transition from babyhood to adulthood in the Orthodox Church is so smooth that the child accepts his Church membership as naturally as he accepts his family relationship. But in the West, Church membership carries with it certain tasks which he must work for and pass. The Western child is conscious that he must struggle to break into the adult world, in the Church as well as in the Society outside. ('Christian Upbringing in East and West'. Article from SOBORNOST June 1943).

97. There is of course a great deal to be said on the other side, as indeed the Orthodox author recognises, but the emphasis on the experienced reality of membership of the Christian community from birth to adulthood as the basis for nurture is one we in Britain need. The strength of the Orthodox position lies in the practice of giving the whole rite of initiation to children within weeks or months of birth so that children are communicating members of the church almost from birth. In the West practice differs between Churches. In the Roman Catholic Church children baptised in infancy are admitted to Holy Communion at about the age of seven and are confirmed about the age of twelve. In the Church of England entry to Holy Communion is by Confirmation which is administered at varying ages, the most common being around thirteen. In Churches of the Reformed tradition there are variations in practice but it has been usual to reserve Holy Communion for Church members and entry into full membership is for adults.

98. Some traditions have said, in effect, that the sacramental life of the Church is adult, and that taking seriously the needs and development of children necessitates a separate structure where living worship is experienced at the child's level of understanding. Such a structure (e.g. the Sunday School or Junior Church) therefore prepares the child for adult worship.

99. Others would argue that the presence of children at the very centre of Christian worship, with the whole worshipping community, is essential, and that participation in such worship is not the *goal* of Christian nurture but the very *means* of nurture. To separate children from the community in worship and make special provision for them is to bring them up in something less than the fulness of Christian experience, and will impoverish their nurture. The sharing of mystery, awe and joy, which should be the experience of worship, is itself a formative experience, part of nurture, and whatever else also needs to be done for a particular age group, to exclude them here is to deny them the fulness of their heritage and to ignore the most effective means of nurture.

100. The gulf between the Church and society, and the fact that the Church is now a religious minority in a pluralist society, means that the ceremonies of the Church are no longer the social rites of passage they once were. It is not only the children of believing parents who present problems for nurture, but those who at various ages and from widely different backgrounds, Christian, semi-Christian and non-Christian, enter the Church. It is much more likely that we cannot conceive of nurture in terms of one systematic process but rather that we must think in terms of all kinds of agencies within the Church which in turn will reflect a much more dynamic and diversified community life, with a much greater willingness to experiment than is usual.

NURTURE FOR DECISION

101. It is all too easy to think of Christian nurture in protective terms, shielding the child from certain experiences and influences and ensuring others, so that at the end of the tunnel a permanent place in the Christian community is assured.

102. The aim of Christian nurture, however, is to enable the child in the end to face a radical challenge. The nurturer must have a real choice in mind: belief or disbelief. This choice initially is presented as part of the child's own development when in early adolescence ability to handle abstract ideas enables him to refine his beliefs by critical examination. It is often pointed out that just as the emergence of religious insights become a real possibility, negative attitudes engendered by previous religious upbringing lead to hostility and rejection.

103. However smooth the passage from birth to adult life, there can be no real personal belief in any depth until it can be called 'my belief', and this pre-supposes a proper questioning of what has been received. Christian nurture must prepare for this and not try to avoid it.

104. There is no doubt that belonging to a religious community is often associated with more positive religious attitudes, though testing of attitudes suggest that church association has less effect than most people within the Churches think. The nature of modern life, however, especially its mobility, makes a continuous holding operation by attachment to a particular Christian community even less certain. Those who work with students or with young adults who leave home to pursue their employment know only too well that once a community tie of long-standing is broken, all too often belief is too shallow to survive. It seems likely that preparation for such a break is often much earlier than the break itself. The crucial time will be around the age of twelve, when the crisis is, or is not, prepared for, though the occasion of crisis may not come until the time of leaving home. The moment of real decision must be prepared for by a rigorous and challenging form of nurture rather than an over protective one.

NURTURE FOR LIFE IN THE WORLD

105. A definition of the aim of the Christian nurture such as 'a building up into the life of the Church' may be criticised as being far too narrow, and, as already suggested, in terms of shepherding the sheep in protective custody. A definition such as 'preparation for life in the world' would be a more acceptable aim. But such contrast is to misunderstand the nature of the Church and to fail to see nurture in the context of the Church's mission to the world. (See para. 69).

106. If Christian nurture is 'in Christ' it is nurture as response to Jesus Christ whose life and work included the life of humanity. Response to him therefore is not in isolation from the world, but, on the contrary, will be embodied in its life and structure. Christian nurture is not for life in the ghetto but for action and participation in society, because the mission of the Church is not something superimposed upon the Church but is inherent in the Gospel which is about the redemption of the world.

107. The Church's relation to society in this country has been so 'established' that its view has been sought on contemporary issues, and these answers have formed the content of so much of our Christian education. Not only does the Church no longer hold this established place and its views are seldom sought, but the problems of modern society do not admit of such treatment. The Church is slowly learning that faith in God is often best expressed in questioning.

108. Nurture as response must have three things in mind.

(a) EXPERIENCE

The structuring of experiencing is part of the process of Christian nurture, but the illumination of that experience into an awareness of God's presence is the activity of grace. This is something we cannot teach, and our nurture patterns must be sensitive to children's religious sensitivity so that the gifts of wonder and awe are preserved. Too often we impose our experience patterns and prevent children from finding their own knowledge of God.

(b) WORLD EVENTS

If we believe God is pressing in upon us in the events of our time, nurture must prepare us for understanding the events of history. As the prophets related their understanding of God's purpose in history to the events of their time, so must we. This is not an individual function outside the context of the Christian community, but a community function which all share. It is essential for understanding and participating in the Church's mission.

(c) PERSONAL ETHICS

The area of moral decision-making is also an area of personal response for which Christian nurture must prepare. It is as we are motivated by our belief in Christ, and as we take our knowledge of him and all his insights about the nature of our humanity into our human relationships that we respond to God's disclosure in Jesus Christ. This is not experienced as a private opinion but happens within the context of the Christian community, yet the decision is personal and constitutes our response. It is not a question of obeying fixed rules, but of responding in given situations as we bring Christians insights to bear on our human behaviour.

Chapter 7

CHRISTIAN NURTURE IN THE LOCAL COMMUNITY

THE FAMILY, THE SCHOOL AND THE CHURCH

109. In the past, because nurture and education have not been identified as separate elements, it has been easy to give to the country day school and to the Church, through its Sunday schools, the same aim – the communication of the Christian faith. They have used similar methods, providing teaching about the bible and the Christian faith and conducting acts of worship. If, as we believe, nurture in the faith can only be done within a community of faith, the role of the school and the Church must be seen as distinctive.

NURTURE AND THE COUNTY SCHOOL

110. The county or 'state' school is one among the community's institutions; it is not an arm of the Church. Religious education in county schools must be able to provide a good educational experience for every child, whether his family is Christian, Humanist, Jewish or Muslim. The aim of religious education in the county school should be to help the pupils to understand what religion is and what it would mean to take a religion seriously. This will involve considerable study of other religions, especially at the secondary level, but this does not mean that the religious education syllabus should become merely a superficial study of many religions. If the pupils are to understand what it means to take a religion seriously they will need to study at least one religion in some detail, and in this country the Christian religion will often be given this close study.

111. The central responsibility of the church school is education. It is as educational institutions that the church schools must be assessed, both by the churches which sponsor them and by the secular educational world. It would seem fitting that a thoroughly educational study of religion should form an important part of the curriculum of church schools.

This does not imply however that the church schools may not have a responsibility also in the area of Christian nurture. This, when it is attempted, must not be confused with the religious education programmes; indeed, any work done in Christian nurture in church schools must be in addition to and not instead of their educational work. Many church schools are already well aware of these distinctions, but further progress must be made in exploring and expressing them. (See Recommendation 14.)

112. But the Christian faith involves a great deal more than can properly be given in lessons about it. It is basically a relation of trust in God through Christ which is reflected in relationships with other people. Christians believe that the nature of God was revealed in a human life, the life of Jesus of Nazareth, and not primarily in the form of statements of belief. What has been true for Christians down the ages is no less true for children now. Children learn about the nature of faith most effectively by seeing it in the lives of the people who matter to them. For young children this means first and foremost their parents.

THE FAMILY AS A UNIT FOR CHRISTIAN NURTURE

113. In the life of the family children can *experience* self-sacrificing love, forgiveness, reconciliation, acceptance, wholeness, which can give positive content to the words of Christian doctrinal statements. Out of such experience come the opportunities to use words to identify beliefs. For children under ten, this is most valuable when done on an individual basis. Children's questions arise spontaneously and should be dealt with as they arise. Their questions are often so profound and difficult ('Why did God make germs?', 'How can Jesus be God if he prayed for God?') that it is difficult to give answers. Yet in the context of family life, discussion can begin, and the child's puzzlement can be freed from anxiety in the context of his parents' love of God. Parents are likely to be able to discover what a child's question really means because they know the child's temperament, his earlier experience, his present hopes and fears, and know that what could be said to one child in the family would be quite wrong if it was said to another. Here too, bible stories can have greater meaning. They become associated in the child's mind with the life of the family and erroneous ideas are likely to be raised in conversation, when they can be discussed within the security of the family relationship.

114. Many parents feel completely inadequate to take over the task which they regard as belonging to the Church. They should not be expected to assume major responsibility for nurture in the faith without support and encouragement. The Church must recognise the family as the first and natural nurturing group and give specific support to parents in their task.

At the present time there is a great weakness here, not only in the materials available but also in understanding how such help can be given. The Church so often looks at adults and children separately, that it finds immense difficulty in identifying the needs of the family as a whole.

115. This is not to say that the family is the only place where Christian nurture can take place. For the young child it must be foremost, but from the early years and increasingly often beyond that age often, the child needs to find that others besides his own family know the reality of a relationship with God. Here is an important role for the larger Christian community.

NURTURE IN THE CHRISTIAN COMMUNITY

116. Within the larger Church the child sees the wider application of Christian principles and discovers that there are people of all ages who offer him love and security, who receive him, give time to him, and help and support him. Here he finds a wider variety of approaches to his questioning. Here above all he is caught up in the joyousness, mystery and world embracing qualities of corporate worship. As he grows, he takes an increasing part in sharing this corporate life with the community around, and he discovers members of the Christian community in the context of many institutions. Thus he may find fellow Christians, whether pupils or teachers, at school.

117. From the age of about ten, children are ready for more systematic learning than is natural within the family and are ready to explore and discuss in groups. This coincides with the stage in their emotional development when they feel increasingly independent of their parents and turn towards their peer group. They may also be reaching the stage in their intellectual development when they are capable of handling abstract thinking, and they can cope with the doctrinal statements on the Christian faith without too much danger of mis-interpretation and distortion. This is the stage when the *words* the Church uses can be seen to be related to the kinds of experience the children have had, and where organizations within the Church can contribute to the nurturing process.

118. The postponement of this kind of teaching does not mean that the gathered Church should not concern itself directly with the younger children. Children are members of the Church, not just future members. If we ask what makes anyone feel that he 'belongs' to any community we should probably say: a sense of fellowship; a sense of enjoyment, which includes happiness and laughter; a sense of significance, the recognition that one belongs and that one matters; a sense of responsibility, of being given tasks to do, tasks where it really matters if one does not do them properly; and a request for service, being asked to give time and energy in the service of others. Those who are teaching children in the Church should be trying to help children to associate with the Church fellowship, enjoyment, significance, responsibility and service, and not simply as giving 'instruction' in the Christian faith. Where special children's groups are provided these only become effective agents of Christian nurture when their life springs from, is involved in and leads into the life of the whole Christian community.

119. It is not difficult to see how a local Church which offers relationships of this quality can nurture even a child whose parents send him to Sunday school but do not go to church themselves. Each congregation will have to tackle this question in the light of its own situation, but possibilities include church-going parents 'adopting' their own children's friends where these friends belong to non-church-going families, church members taking responsibility for neighbours' children, and members of the congregation acting as 'family' for church activities or for being together in services of

41

worship. Experience has shown that where parents are actively involved in the Christian nurture of their children, more of them will take part in church life themselves. Most parents care about the welfare of their children, but in the traditional organization of the Church's education programme, they seldom feel needed. (See paragraph 41.)

120. The minister or priest plays a key role in enabling the Church to become an effective nurturing community. He himself must be a group member, not acting alone either in pulpit or administration, but as the first among equals in a team. He can do much to enable children as well as adults to know the community's need of them. He can help the lay leaders to become sensitive to individuals and groups, so that they set the pattern in their own relationships. (See Recommendation 2.)

NURTURING GROUPS WITHIN THE CHURCH

121. A nurturing group consists of any group of adults among whom the child is accepted, cared for and involved. It is important that the child feels needed as much as any other member of the group.

In many cases children and young people will choose clubs, uniformed organizations and other groups in which they meet their peers, but in every case the adult leadership is crucial, if the group is not to be isolated from the rest of the Christian community, but feel itself an integral part of it. This is most likely to happen when the members identify their purpose with that of the Church, often in relation to a particular project, e.g. preparing a special act of worship, helping to raise money, or contributing to a concert.

122. Such occasions often break down age barriers completely. Redecorating an old person's room may involve older children and adults together, while even the younger children help with fetching and carrying. In fact such a project may become the special concern of an enlarged family group, into which lone adults and children whose parents are not in the church are drawn together with a family. Very often even young children make friends with an older person who sits near them during worship, so that new 'families' are formed. Such groupings may arise from the traditional Sunday school class, where a teacher and her family or friends are regularly joined by one or two children during worship. A Church alert to this kind of development could make further use of the situation. For instance, groups in turn might be asked to prepare the intercessions, or take on the care of a housebound member of the community.

123. Real situations like these are less formal than most contrived teaching situations, and more easily seen to be related to life. They thus provide opportunities for shared experiences which are the essence of Christian nurture. Some Churches consciously look for experiences which can be shared by the whole community, in which age and family boundaries are enlarged, and opportunities made for relationships to be formed and

deepened. Such, for example, might be family week-end conferences, and other occasions when the Eucharist takes place in the context of a total programme which includes Sunday lunch or the occasional Saturday party.

124. What is the place of the Sunday school in all this? Clearly the traditional 'Sunday school movement' has little in this concept of nurture, since it tended to function as a separate entity merely attached to the local church. But although much growing and learning takes place when all ages are together, there must often be opportunity for particular age groups to work at their own pace in relation to their own level of understanding. This need not mean, however, that there are always firm demarcation lines between age groups, nor that there should be regular pattern of groups such as the traditional Sunday school tended to provide. The oldest and the youngest in the Church may sometimes find great value in meeting together, as may the adolescents and the adults. Older children may have prepared a programme to share with younger ones, and on another occasion all-age groups may be the right mixture. For each purpose, the leadership needs to be chosen according to that particular circumstance, perhaps from a pool of those able to help, having been suitably trained in leadership skills, or having special abilities to offer. Some groups may find occasional projects, each lasting for a specified number of weeks, preferable to an indefinitely prolonged series of lessons or to an annual cycle of study.

IMPLICATIONS FOR THE LIFE AND STRUCTURE OF THE LOCAL CHURCH

125. If Christian nurture is taken seriously, the whole life of the Church must be reappraised. Questions must be asked about its essential ethos and the relationships which form it. Is this a community which proclaims in action the faith of which it speaks in words? How is the stranger, adult or child, received? What natural groupings exist and is there communication between them or could they be described as cliques? How much is this community aware of the real needs of those around it and within it?

126. Nurturing includes the offering of security and community tradition, but it should not do this to the exclusion of independent or even revolutionary thought and action. To be able to question the norms of the Christian community without breaking the relationship is of prime importance. Children will achieve this balance if in the community where they feel most accepted and at home they find adults who question traditional ways and are capable of responding to new situations with novel actions.

Going to Church - Judith Hayes 5 yrs

PART TWO: UNDERSTANDING CHRISTIAN NURTURE

Chapter 8

CHRISTIAN NURTURE IN AN OPEN SOCIETY

127. In the next five chapters an attempt is made to develop a theology of critical openness as an important part of an understanding of Christian nurture and growth. We do not pretend this is a full treatment of the nature of Christian nurture and we do not think 'critical openness' is at all times and in all places its most important aspect. Love is greater. But we do believe it has great significance for the process of Christian growth in modern Western societies and it is because we have found ourselves asking what it means to foster Christian faith in such societies (especially in Britain) that our attention has been drawn to 'critical openness' as a vital key in unlocking the problems and in opening the way to a renewed and more confident policy of Christian nurture for the churches.

128. What are the practical ramifications of a policy of critical openness in Christian nurture? Chapters 13, 14 and 15 look at the process of Christian nurture in the two important areas of family and worship. A third area is the school but we feel the Christian presence in our day schools is too large a subject for treatment in this report although in Appendix I we have made some observations about Christian nurture in Christian schools. Finally in Appendix II we have listed a few of the important areas which we feel need attention but which we have had to omit from our considerations.

CRITICAL OPENNESS AND CHRISTIAN NURTURE

129. Armed with the idea of critical openness let us return to the situation in which Christian nurture exists side by side with secular education. The education of the young child emphasises discovery, exploration, stimulating and directing the child's curiosity. The older pupil is to become critically aware of his own beliefs and values. He is encouraged to look at evidence, to give reasons and to think for himself. Secular education and Christian nurture share the same spirit of critical openness but they differ in their goals, the latter seeking to deepen Christian life and faith whilst the former is compatible with a wide range of religious and non-religious attitudes. In educational discussion critical openness is usually called autonomy.

130. Christian nurture, as the process of learning and growing which intends to deepen Christian faith, once had a dominant position, if not a virtual monopoly of the learning situations in Britain. Christian learning was the main model of learning, and this situation continued even after the state entered education in its own rights in 1870. For most of the century which followed, the church, the church school and the county or state school were in partnership as offering Christian nurture. Today all that is changed. Secular education has come of age. The study of education, through its branches such as educational psychology, philosophy and sociology, has now generated a wide range of theories of education and models of schooling, and the process of Christian nurture, once taken for granted, is now exposed as but one amongst many processes and types of learning. Christian nurture can appear to be rather parochial, rather narrow, offering only constricted horizons to young people, while secular education presents itself as open, all-embracing, allied with scientific discovery, able, through a multitude of techniques and aids, to offer the widest opportunities to all. Will not Christian nurture seem to be concerned with its own survival rather than with the genuine well being of the young? May it not even appear to be a process of indoctrination?

131. Not only is our society marked by various patterns of learning, most of which are secular, but it is increasingly varied religously. Most religious groups seem to have found the relativity and the comparisons which are implied by their living side by side an embarassment. Various ways of dealing with this may be seen, ranging from the attempt to establish dominance over the society, to a virtual withdrawal from society. In the plural cities of the Middle East (and of Belfast) communities are geographically divided along religious lines. This certainly simplifies the problem of transmission of an undiluted religious heritage. In most Western countries we find a proliferation of religious sects, marked by their vigorous proselytism, removing the young convert from his family or secluding him from society entirely for a time. The sectarian patterns of instruction tend to be very authoritarian, with an emphasis on obedient acceptance of the doctrines of the movement, teaching certain standard replies to objections, and training in how to ward off criticism. One can see the advantage of these methods. They seem likely to prevent the movement from suffering from competition, and to increase the coherence of the movement and its hold over its young people.

132. But wnat should be the policy of the main Christian churches in these matters? Generally speaking, particularly in recent years, the ecumenical churches have been uneasy about closed authoritarian instruction, and have often adopted a policy of deliberate openness towards each other and the various surrounding religious and educational movements. But is there not some risk that the open approach will mean that our young people and children will be lost to less scrupulous bodies? And do not young people develop with greater confidence when protected? Does not the very word 'nurture' suggest a degree of secluded protection? (See para 199). And what

is the rationale in theology itself for a Christian nurture which would be non-authoritarian and open to other views?

133. Critical openness is the central idea in the resolution of these problems. It is the main feature which distinguishes the faith-fostering activities of the main-stream churches from those of the sects. Without an understanding of this, there is no satisfactory way in which Christian upbringing in open, plural societies can be defended against the charge that it is indoctrinatory, and without the practice of critical openness there is no way whereby Christian adults can be formed so as to live freely and creatively in plural societies (see paras. 150 and 200).

134. The Christian life is not the only form of the educated life, and it would be a mistake think that being educated and becoming Christian are the same. On the other hand, being brought up as a Christian or being nurtured as a Christian *is* the same as becoming a better Christian. So while education and Christian nurture share the spirit of critical openness, they differ in their goals, the latter seeking to deepen Christian life and faith whilst the former is compatible with quite a wide range of religious and non-religious attitudes.

Summary: Christian nurture is like the closed and dogmatic instruction of the Christian sects in that its content is the Christian faith and its object the deepening of that faith but it differs in that it possesses the spirit of critical openness. It is similar to secular education in placing a high value on critical openness but differs in that it deliberately seeks to deepen Christian faith.

CRITICAL OPENNESS AND AUTONOMY

135. The expressions 'critical openness' and 'autonomy' are similar but not identical. Both describe the one who thinks for himself, and both agree that this is not to be confused with thinking what one likes. A person who thinks for himself in mathematics has freedom with the concepts he is using and may even be creative with them. He is their master because he understands them. But they have also mastered him. He is under their discipline, and he cannot just think what he likes about them. It is because the ideas of autonomy and critical openness emphasise the importance of understanding reasons that this distinction is made between thinking for oneself and thinking that someone (whether yourself or someone else) happens to like to think.

136. Another similarity between critical openness and autonomy is that the two ideas each imply a process of growth, or are states achieved during or after growth. Educational philosophers and psychologists have often discussed the obstacles to autonomy, and the means of fostering its early appearance. Growth is necessary not only to attain autonomy but also to maintain it. Autonomy may be lost not only to others but to my own past self. If my past self so directs my thinking as to stop me from responding with suitable creativity to the problems of today, I have become heteronomous – ruled by another self, my own past self.

137. Although, as we have seen, being autonomous requires one to be open to the call of reason, and in that sense to stand under the discipline of reason, this aspect of the idea is more obvious in the expression 'critical openness'. To be open is to listen, to be ready to receive other persons, to hear new ideas, to re-examine one's own past, whereas autonomy could perhaps suggest a certain isolation, even a self-enclosed independence, or it might suggest individualism, whereas critical openness is intended to suggest that one is in a community, a learning community, in which one both speaks and listens, being both critical and receptive. A pre-requisite of learning is humility. You must recognise that there is something to be learned and that it may be worth learning. The term 'critical openness' suggests better than the term 'autonomy' this humility and this probing towards the unknown.

KNOWLEDGE AND VALUES

138. The expression 'critical openness' has another advantage. The things which exist to be known are more important than the satisfactions they give us in knowing them. The objects of knowledge have what we might call a primacy of value over the various values which knowing selves derive from their knowledge, like a feeling of fulfilment. This view of knowledge is not confined to Christians and it can be defended on purely philosophical grounds, but it is consistent with Christian faith, and indeed, seems to be required by it. God is glorified because he is God, not because praising him gives the believer a sense of wellbeing. He is trusted because he is worthy of trust, not because such trust secures salvation. Just so, if we take this view, the world itself is to be investigated not mainly because such investigation is useful, or satisfying, or tending to produce certain ethical qualities, but because it is marvellous. In the end, it is that which makes the investigation satisfying and gives it its ethical qualities.

139. Again, history is to be studied not primarily because of its contemporary relevance, or its character-building effects but because man himself is worthy of study, and the study of history is a love of the human past, not seen merely as a curiosity, but as a critical and self-critical brotherly interest and respect for the people of the past. Now, the idea of autonomy usually takes the form of announcing conditional regulations for the living of the rational life: 'In as much as one believes, feels and acts, one should do so truthfully, reasonably.' We may contrast this view, which states how one should live *to the extent* that one decides to live that way, with the view which declares that we *ought* to actively pursue new knowledge, ought to seek truth, ought to follow hard after beauty, because they demand this of us. The latter view could be called 'open rationality'. It is clearly close to Christian faith, and has affinities with the Christian virtues of faith, hope and love. While the word autonomy could express these emphases, the term 'critical openness' is a more effective way of highlighting them.

Summary: Critical openness and autonomy are similar ideas in that both describe the life which is lived freely and reasonably rather than blindly in habit, convention or mere obedience; but critical openness suggests interdependence, receptivity, and a loving, listening attitude. It is thus closer to Christian faith.

CRITICAL OPENNESS AND THE NEW TESTAMENT

140. Critical openness is also related to the New Testament image of the Christian life. 'The prophets who prophesied of the grace that was to be yours searched and inquired about this salvation. They inquired what person or time was indicated by the Spirit of Christ within them' (1 Peter 1:10-1). The prophets are certainly not thought of here as examining the evidence of their prophecies to see if it was credible or not. Rather, they made a spiritual and perhaps mystical search into the inner meaning to discover the truth hidden there. The sense is similar to John 5:39, where the Jews are spoken of as searching the scriptures. The Beroean Jews (Acts 17:11) displayed a spirit of enquiry which was possibly closer to that which we meet today, when they 'received the word with all eagerness, examining the scriptures daily to see if these things were so.' When the Spirit of God or Christ is described as 'searching' the reference is a searching out and bringing to light of what is already known, a probing or testing, as when Christ searches the mind and hearts of men (Relevelation 2:23), or 'The Spirit searches everything, even the depths of God' (1 Corinthians 2:10), but when this searching Spirit dwells in the hearts of believers, he enables them to search out what they did *not* know before, giving them spiritual insight and discerning power. So 'The spiritual man judges all things, but is himself to be judged by none' (1 Corinthians 2:15). The penetrating power of the Spirit is spoken of in Romans 8:26-27, where human ignorance of what to pray for is overcome by the searching knowledge of the Spirit, too deep for words. This power of penetrating enquiry is to be turned outwards, as when Christians are advised to 'test the spirits', to see whether they are of God' (1 John 4:1) and inwards, as when the Corinthian Christians were told 'Examine yourselves, to see whether you are holding to your faith. Test yourselves' (2 Corinthians 13:5).

141. The gift of discrimination is impelled by the knowledge of God's discrimination (his judgement) between men. 'If we judged ourselves truly, we should not be judged. When we are judged by the Lord we are chastened, so that we may not be condemned along with the world' (1 Corinthians 11:31f). It is because the judgement of the Lord is expressed through his giving of himself in the bread and the wine (1 Corinthians 11:27) that Christians are not only to examine themselves before they partake but also to discern the body of the Lord (vv 28f). We can see that the critical and discriminating spirit of the early Church sprang thus not only from the Old Testament doctrine of the all-searching eye of God but also from the peculiar tension of the early

Christian community, caught between a given salvation and a not yet given vindication. It is this situation of being poised on the brink of a great crisis, of being granted complete certainty, yet enjoying it in uncertainty, which gave the Christian critical spirit its essential flavour. On the other hand, 'there is no condemnation' (Romans 8:1) and on the other hand, 'the time has come for judgement to begin with the household of God' (1 Peter 4:17). Certainly, there are times when this critical spirit of testing is to be suspended. When the Corinthian Christians sit down to dinner, they are not to ask questions about the food set before them, just for conscience sake, but to eat it up in the name of faith (1 Corinthians 10:25,27), and Paul acknowledges the limits of self-knowledge and self-criticism. 'It is a very small thing that I should be judged by you or by any human court. I do not even judge myself' (1 Corinthians 4:3). The key thought is that it is ultimately God who is the supreme tester and validator of hearts. 'It is the Lord who judges me' (1 Corinthians 4:4).

CRITICISM AND THE COMING KINGDOM

142. This inquiring spirit of the early Church may be called 'eschatological criticism'. It springs from a knowledge that the goal has not yet been grasped (Philippians 3:12), the future not yet known (1 John 3:2), the true and the false grow side by side (Matthew 13:30). Everything therefore was to be tested, and that which survived the test was to be held fast. 'You judge according to the flesh. I judge no one. Yet even if I do judge, my judgment is true, for it is not I alone that judge, but I and he who sent me' (John 8:15-16). The opposing poles of human error and divine insight are brought together in the church, which is in the world, and therefore cannot assess, and is in the Spirit, and therefore assesses everything.

143. The criticism which we have seen to be so marked a feature of the early Christian existence sprang from the ambiguities which this situation posed. Were the prophets true or false (1 John 4:5)? Were the miracles those of Christ or anti-Christ (2 Thess. 2:9-12)? Satan himself appears as an angel of light. One must always be vigilant, always watchful, ready for constant examination (Luke 12:35-40). The stress on this was part of the 'instruction of the Lord' (Eph. 6:4), part of his chastening, by means of which suffering itself was part of the lesson which disclosed the truth (Heb. 12:3-11), and made the whole Christian life one of discipleship in the school of Christ (Matt. 11:29; 13:52).

144. In some senses, there were limits to this spirit of criticism. The question was which was the wheat and which the tares, not whether there was any wheat. It was a matter of when and where the Christ would come, not whether. And yet, in another sense, there were no limits, for the situation was one from which only the 'end' would bring any escape (1 Thess. 5:1-11). Until the day when the perfect came, the believer just had to go on, peering into the dark mirror (1 Corinthians 13:12). It was radical in that the tension between the old age and the new age was absolute. It was the doubt and the

criticism which belonged to the Kingdom, the seed growing secretly (Mark4:26-29). The critical doubt was itself an expression of life in the Kingdom (Luke 12:54-59), since it sprang out of the perception that the Kingdom was, and yet was not yet. The critical testing of all things was a demand of Christian obedience (Mark 13:5-6). It was directed to the uncertainties, but it sprang from the certainties (Mark 13:32-36). Any child growing up into the Kingdom would have to grow up through that testing, being examined and learning to examine. But this was easy, because of the nature of the child and the nature of the Kingdom. For unless the Kingdom was received as a little child, it could not be entered (Mark 10:15). For the child such learning is natural, and it is also the nature of the Kingdom to consist of such learners.

Summary: The concept of Christian criticism although related to and affected by many modern trends, springs essentially from the New Testament where it is one mark of the eschatological people of God.

CHRISTIAN NURTURE AND A PLURAL SOCIETY

145. Christian nurture is offered by Christians to Christians in order to strengthen Christian faith and to develop Christian character. Christian nurture is easily distinguished from general education, including religious education as carried on in state schools, since the latter does not *intend* (see para. 188) to build up Christian faith (although like any other worthwhile activity it may have this effect) nor *must* the teachers of general education, including religious education, be Christians, although they *may* be. Moreover, general education is offered to all. It is possible but not necessary to base general education on Christian faith but it is necessary that Christian nurture should spring from and be defined by Christian faith (see para. 189). The distinction is important but the words which express it may vary. It is quite possible to call 'Christian nurture' 'Christian education' and to mean by the latter term the whole of the Christian upbringing process, but the disadvantage of this terminology is that it may carry the implicatiuon that general education is positively or even necessarily non-Christian. It is to avoid this confusion that the expression 'Christian nurture' is used.

146. Grasping the point of the distinction depends to some extent on acknowledging that there is an 'outside' with respect to the Church, a realm of human culture and expertise, which pursues its own goals. These goals are to be distinguished from the obvious or immediate goals of church life but they are not necessarily hostile to the church, and may be 'outside' only in the sense that they are ruled by their own logic. So we have such human enterprises as science, medicine, the fine arts and education. Whatever the relations between such pursuits and the institutionalised church as well as the Christian gospel (and these relations are of many kinds, often intimate and subtle) nevertheless they cannot be reduced to ecclesiastical or theological

pursuits simply and without remainder. So in order to see the point of the Christian nurture/secular education distinction it is necesary to recognise that Christian faith exists in a plural world, plural not only culturally but intellectually and conceptually. Thus it becomes one thing to seek or intend to bring up one's children as Christians within the church and another thing (not better or worse but different) to seek to educate them vocationally, culturally and intellectually for life in the world. These two activities will of course be related in all sorts of ways; the point is simply that they can be distinguished as well as related and that to some degree the formation of the church's policy in Christian nurture will be shaped by the recognition of the difference.

147. It may also be that perception of the Christian nurture/secular education distinction is coloured by traditional Christian background. The Catholic Church, for instance, has never relinquished to the state its own prerogative as educator of the people, and possesses an integrated parish and day school system combining both Christian nurture and general education. For many Catholics therefore the distinction may seem unreal, or inapplicable to their own situation, or even misleading and dangerous. For the Free Churches, the right of the state to educate has long been granted, but individuals and churches may differ in the degree to which it is realised that secular education is a more or less independent sphere of activity, and they may also differ about the degree to which the distinction is a good thing or a bad thing. For many Free Church people the perception of the Christian nurture/secular education difference is a matter of how to construe the presence of Christian faith in the world, and so a matter of how to understand mission, especially mission in a secularised and highly specialised society. The Anglican Church occupies an intermediate position and exhibits both kinds of response.

148. Christian nurture, especially of children, is made more problematic by the fact that it is, in Britain, taking place in a society in which the models of learning are controlled by secular education (see para. 130). It is probably true that the reaction of most religious groups to the relativising pressures of pluralism has been to create special, segregated residential areas. No doubt the Christian, Jewish and Muslim quarters of cities in the Middle East are not only culturally and linguistically convenient but also simplify the passing on of religious belief (see para. 131). But such religious apartheid is ill at ease with the mobility, the mass communications and the common schools of the western democracies. In a society in which education at its best insists that everything is to be examined, how can a process in which some things are not to be examined (if this is indeed the situation of Christian nurture) escape inferior status and moral reproach (Is it then the case that Christian nurture does have affinities with anti-autonomous and conformist processes? If Christians were content, as some seem to be, to let education have a monopoly of critical openness and to allow Christian nurture to be assimilated into Christian instruction or even Christian (*sic*) indoctrination, the problem of the relation of critical openness to Christian nurture would be solved simply

by denying that critical openness has any place in Christian nurture.

149. But then *either* Christian parents think that critical openness is bad for everyone's children,
or they think it good for other people's children but bad for their own,
or they think it good for other people's children and good for their own except in the area of their religous development. The first position would mean the breakdown of the Christian enterprise within modern secular education and the triumph, within the churches, of authoritarian instruction. The second position is not much better; indeed, it seems less consistent, and would lead to Christians continuing to support enquiring education in the public sector but withdrawing their own children. But in some ways, the last position is the worst of all, since the young Christian is now given to understand that he may think for himself in every area except that which is expected to be his deepest commitment. Such a policy will not attract worthwhile young people for more than a few years, nor will it deserve to.

150. If Christian nurture were to be collapsed into Christian instruction the idea of being a Christian person would also have changed. Just as education, instruction, socialisation, indoctrination and so on imply different views of man, so Christian nurture, Christian instruction, Christian training and so on imply different views of Christian man. Are Christians to be conformist, passive acceptors of authority, unable to adapt to crises, too set in the received ways to think creatively? Only a Christian nurtured in critical openness can have characteristics other than these (see para. 133). For those who think that this *other* Christian life is essential for the continued vitality and relevance of Christian faith, the problem of how Christian nurture is deliberately to promote Christian life and faith while possessing critical openness is a central concern.

Summary: Although the distinction between general education and Christian nurture is clear and important, the element of critical openness cannot be confined to general education, but must be part of a specifically Christian upbringing. Difficult although this may seem, the alternatives are even more discouraging.

Daniel in the Lions' Den - Alice Park 6 yrs

Chapter 9

CRITICAL OPENNESS AND FAITH

151. In our discussion of the New Testament elements in the concept of critical openness (paras. 140-144), it was pointed out that testing, careful investigation, diligent enquiry and other New Testament ideas which are similar to our idea of critical openness sprang not accidentally but inevitably from the early Church's understanding of its position between two ages. It would be natural to suppose that the fusion of the Greek spirit of intellectual enquiry with the Hebrew-Christian traditions which took place during the development of patristic theology would have heightened this aspect of Christian living still more, and made self-criticism and open scrutiny of others a strong element in the Christian tradition. This does not seem to have happened in quite this simple manner. Such passages as 1 Timothy 1:3-8; 6:3-4; 2 Timothy 2:2-9; Titus 1:9-11 and 2 Peter 2 suggest that even before the end of the Apostolic Age an authoritarian conservatism was beginning to harden the arteries of the church. Such wide-ranging minds as those of Clement of Alexandria and Origen are to be found, but often the history of Christian thought shows that a period of creative criticism is followed by a time of sterile scholasticism, and this phenomenon is not confined to theology. The European Church in the sixteenth century presents a remarkable example of Christian self-criticism, but often one gets the impression that in spite of a profound reappraisal of the foundations of Christian faith the resulting doctrinal systems were taught with majestic authority, as if they themselves were immune to the searching criticism which they devoted to other Christian systems.

152. Not until the late eighteenth and nineteenth centuries, with the rise of biblical criticism and the appearance of such self-critical theologies of culture as that of Friedrich Schleiermacher, does the glory of the Christian critical spirit emerge again. But by then, it was almost too late. Certain assumptions about the nature of Christian faith had gathered such strength that they had become almost instinctive to the ordinary Christian mind (see para. 175). In the many works written in Britain during the first thirty years of the twentieth century which dealt with the problem of introducing the criticism of the Bible to school-children, we can see some of the first attempts to reintroduce the critical spirit into the programmes of Christian instruction and nurture which the churches were providing in the schools. The problem-centred method of teaching religious education and the experimental approaches of the 1960s also represented adaptations of Christian nurture to the demands of a critical and exploratory secular education, but during the 1970s there was something of a relapse, many churches returning to more authoritarian kinds of teaching emphasising passivity, acceptance and obedience. The early Christian

vision of examination has been splendidly restored in contemporary theology, but it is vital for the faith nurturing programmes of the churches today that it be restored to the Christian nurture and upbringing of children and especially to lay education within the churches.

153. Several areas of Christian faith and life now seem at first sight to be ill at ease with the spirit of Christian critical openness. These include the idea of the finality of Christian faith, and certain aspects of Christian spirituality. But is it true that these areas are really hostile to critical openness? Might not an examination show that in fact they impel the Christian towards autonomy and criticism?

Summary: Although it is not always evident, the critical spirit of Christian faith reappears from time to time. But it is often felt to be ill at ease with such areas as revelation and the divine authority.

THE FINALITY OF FAITH

154. If the Christian faith is final and perfect, how can it require or be amenable to self-criticism? Sometimes an attempt is made to make room for criticism by distinguishing between finality in principle and the actual state of the faith, which is still in progress. In Catholicism, this sometimes takes the form of belief in a gradual unfolding, such that the essentials are present from the start, their implications being consistently unpacked with the passage of time. In its Protestant form, the usual idea is that the actual life and faith of the church is criticised in the light of the Bible, which is idealised as the pure deposit of revealed faith, the final truth to which the actual church is always being summoned and by which it is judged.

155. Whether in its Catholic or Protestant form, this approach does make some room for Christian criticism. The actual church, for example, can be judged by the ideal of the essential church, the church as it most truly is. Or (to take another example) if the true faith is gradually being developed, or gradually being realised, then we need to have in our minds some of the norms or marks of the true faith, so that we can see whether they are present in any situation of the actual church which claims to be a fuller realisation of the Gospel. But then these norms or marks will have to be discussed and given their relative weight, and the criteria for selecting them rather than others will have to be set out. All this will demand a critical approach towards the faith itself, not only in its actual but in its ideal or essential form.

156. But problems remain. Does the kind of approach we have outlined give the Christian sufficient ground for criticising the essentials themselves? Is there not some risk that the very distinction between the real faith and the actual faith, the former being used as a standard by which to assess the latter, will tend to leave the true faith unpurged? Surely the distinction between the real and the actual will itself tend to breakdown. If we investigate the 'marks'

of the true faith, some may be found to be less eternal, and so might be moved from the 'real' class into the 'actual' class. And indeed the history of theology presents us with many cases of shifts of this kind. In the last resort, in spite of its frequent usefulness, this approach to the problem of reconciling finality and criticism seems likely to become a device for restraining criticism of the central features and confining it to criticism of peripheral matters. The idea then becomes to hold fast to the Bible and criticise everything else. But the Christian principle of self-criticism must flow from the whole of the Christian faith and not be exercised against some aspect on the initiative of some other aspect. Christian criticism cannot rest content with a sort of content division within Christian faith. It must flow from the whole and react against the whole.

THE FINALITY OF RELIGIOUS EXPERIENCE

A second possible approach would be to distinguish the finality of experience from the finality of thought. The idea of the finality of the work of Christ can refer to its experienced religious adequacy. I may find that tomorrow I am even more deeply satisfied. That would not carry the implication that yesterday my satisfaction was less than complete for me as I was then. I may grow in my capacity for experiencing the profound beauty of the cross of Christ, without ever being conscious of dissatisfaction. In this sense, finality and development are compatible. The last coach on the train is always final, regardless of the speed of the train. But if I articulate my experience in propositions, *i.e.* if I theologise about it, then my cognitions of today may be in tension with those of yesterday and I may have to choose. Perhaps this distinction between experienced finality (the lack of any experience of religious dissatisfaction) and reflective infinality (the knowledge that sharper and clearer expression may show me that I was at least partly wrong in *speaking* about it the way I did yesterday) may help to define the nature of critical openness in relation to the finality and perfection of the Christian faith.

158. The distinction between experienced and articulated finality does however have its limits. Can experience and reflection be so neatly distinguished? Does not the distinction lead me to be critically open towards the thoughts of others but self-enclosed as far as my experience goes? Does it not fail to open me to the *experience* of others? And may I not delude myself about my experience, thinking I was satisfied when I was not, or attributing my satisfaction to this when later I realise it was that which was the true source of my satisfaction? Is there not some danger of absolutising experience, so that while I may criticise yesterday's theology, I may never theologically criticise yesterday's religious experience, or today's? It is not easy to see how this approach can be defended any better than the last one from the suspicion that in the end it can become a way for limiting the operation of critical openness.

COGNITIVE FINALITY

159. In discussing the problem of critical openness towards the future of the child, we remarked that the Christian nurturer knows what he is nurturing his children out of, but not what he is nurturing them into. 'They know the resources but not the use which will be made of them' (para. 63). This conception could be compatible with either of the two views discussed above. But whereas we there suggest the metaphor of the paintbox, the metaphor of the hidden time capsule might attract some. Christian faith may be misleadingly regarded as a capsule full of items hidden by Christ and the early Church two thousand years ago. We are learning how to unlock the compartments, and to draw out new items, not knowing what impact they will have upon us or our Christian future. But the truth is more complex. The past of Christian faith is not protected from its environment in a time capsule, to be opened by us, to find each thing as it was when first stored away. The past of Christian faith is available to us only in language and ritual. Both are inescapably embedded in culture, and demand constant re-interpretation. No doubt the past is just exactly whatever it was. But we do not know what it was, and as we make it *our* past, our perceptions of it also change. Not only do we not know for what future we are nurturing our young Christians; we do not fully know from what past we are nurturing them. Their perceptions of the Christian past may be as different from ours as ours are from the generation of Christians who lived before form criticism. And just as individuals may have false experience, self-deluding experience, only recognised and corrected in the light of a later wholeness, so whole communities and traditions may pass through perods of mistaken experience. What else are prophets for but to awaken people to this?

THE FINALITY OF CHRIST

160. Another and perhaps more promising alternative is that we should seek to apply and extend the early Christian idea of the eschatological ambiguity of the church's life as an impulse to examine everything carefully (paras. 149-144). Christian faith has finality and completeness within it but this is perceived according to the promise, by faith and hope. The perfect future, as and when it is realised, can be seen, looking back, to be the product of the past. But to one looking forward, the future shape cannot be easily extrapolated from the present or the past. We strain our minds and eyes with eager expectation, looking, wondering, trying to discern the signs, trying to discriminate between the false and the true, looking for the emerging reality (Romans 8:19; Phil. 3:13), which is Christ. Christ is the centre of critical openness for the Christian, not only in so far as he is the model which we imitate in his earthly ministry (paras. 170 and 177), but he in so far as he is the one who is still to come. This form of theological or eschatological finality is also connected with the doctrine of justification by faith (paras. 179 and 180). It does express an experienced reality, for living with the criticism which is

a mark of the ambiguous in-between age affects the way life is experienced, seen and felt, but it must be emphasised that fundamentally one must describe this finality in theological terms not psychological. But the eschatological ambiguity leads us straight into the problem of authority.

Summary: We have discussed four kinds of finality: that of principle or essence, experienced finality, cognitive finality and the finality of the end which is present and for which we still wait. The last view seems most promising for the theology of Christian nurture.

CRITICAL OPENNESS AND AUTHORITY

161. Let us begin our examination of the relation between authority and critical openness by distinguishing the authoritative from the authoritarian. An authoritative view carries authority for certain reasons. Perhaps the knowledge, advice or instruction comes from one who is wise, experienced or loved. Perhaps the counsel is presented with good arguments. But an authoritarian position is so merely by decree. The authoritarian person admits of no criteria for the assessing of his authority) he offers no reasons beyond the command itself. But if there are criteria then they must be examined, compared, ascertained, and the pronouncement itself must also be examined to see whether it meets the requirements of the criteria. So if religious authority is authoritative, then it demands scrutiny by its very nature. But if it is authoritarian, it will brook no criticism, and indeed, criticism could find no starting place. Criteria-referenced authority summons the co-operative effort of the one who stands beneath the authority. But the authoritarian decree is right because of its power alone. The authoritarian person is right because he says so. The authoritarian book is true because it claims to be. Here openness becomes disobedience and criticism is impudence. Of what kind is the authority of God – authoritative or authoritarian?

162. Sometimes an attempt is made to avoid the force of this distinction, and the implications for Christian life which flow from it, by introducing such euphemisms as 'innate authority' or 'self-authenticating authority'. Innate authority is one which acknowledges no criteria. It remains mysterious, baffling, frustrating. 'Why don't you want to go to London?' 'I just don't want to.' 'But *why*?' There is no *reason* why the friend should not change his mind.'Oh, alright. I will go after all.' 'What made you change your mind?' 'I don't know. I just decided to go after all.' You are pleased with the decision, but as mystified as ever. It is not possible to enter into understanding and sympathetic relations with someone whose decisions are arbitrary. This remains true even if, as in the case of God, the danger of unpredictable ethical changes is removed. Such a God could not be the Thou of man; he could not be the counsellor and guide, for to accept such guidance would be to renounce the status of person and to accept the status of slave. You may trust God in the dark, but you cannot trust a dark God.

THE MYSTERY OF GOD

163. The mystery of God is not the mystery of the arbitrary. In front of the merely arbitrary, one can only shrug one's shoulders or resign oneself. The arbitrary repels; it resists attempts to enter it. It is a whimsical, even if the whims are matters of life and death. But the mystery of God is wondrous. It draws one into its depths. One wonders not that there is so little to know but that there is so much to know. It is when the mysterious ways of the Lord have been penetrated to some extent (Romans 9-11) that one cries out in worship, 'O the depth of the riches and wisdom and knowledge of God! How unsearchable are his judgements and how inscrutable his ways!' (Romans 11:33). Here one is walking in the light which penetrates further and further back, into eternity. But a dark God, one whose commands are authoritarian, plunges one into confusion and credulity, whilst himself remaining unrevealed. It is true that not everything in God is discoverable by human reason, but it is equally true that nothing in God plunges reason into dismay.

AUTONOMY, HETERONOMY AND THEONOMY

164. When problems of authority are being discussed, distinctions are sometimes made between autonomy, heteronomy and theonomy. Autonomy is obeying a self-imposed or responsibly recognised rule or standard. Heteronomy is submitting to a law or standard imposed by another. Theonomy is submitting to the law of God. Theonomy, it is sometimes said, differs from heteronomy because it is a voluntary submission. But the same questions which we ask of the distinction between heteronomy and autonomy need to be asked of the concept 'theonomy'. Theonomy can take either an autonomous or a heteronomous form. In its heteronomous form, theonomy is submitting, of my own free will, to a law to which I am invited. But when I submit voluntarily, do I do so for reasons or not? If there are no reasons, how does my submission differ from an arbitrary whim of mine? The attempt to save the Christian doctrine of man by emphasising the voluntary nature of the submission is only partly successful, if it be the case that I voluntarily yield myself by an arbitrary whim. But perhaps it was not a whim. Perhaps I felt constrained. But did I perceive, in the constraint, something which made me believe that it came from God? If so, would not the recognising of that have involved me in the criteria for what comes from God and what does not? And would I not then be on the edge of experiencing the constraint of reasons? On the other hand, if there were no reasons to believe the constraint came from God, then surely the constriant was merely a blind force to which I gave in.

165. It is easy to see that the notion of theonomy can be interpreted in such a way that it becomes merely another name for heteronomy, all the more dangerous because it involves me in submitting to a dark God. But if theonomy is interpreted as autonomy, then it becomes rather like our idea of critical

openness, since it emphasises the virtues of humility and loving listening to God in an alert, thoughtful way. Autonomous theonomy would seek out the nature of God, not his whims, and would seek to distinguish this nature by certain non-subjective norms, whether drawn from history or philosophy or theology or from ethics, and seek to draw up criteria for knowing when the voice was indeed the voice of the Master. We can see therefore that the idea of theonomy, although a valuable idea, cannot be used to avoid the challenge of the distinction between heteronomy and autonomy, but must itself be examined to see to which of these it may be closest.

GOD CALLS US TO CRITICAL OPENNESS

166. The alternatives are clear. Either we have a dictator God, or we are called to the life of critical openness. But God in declaring himself a God for man, in making himself available to us in personal relationship, invites us to accept a reasonable service. Critical openness is the pedagogical technique adopted by a God who is personal and desires us to be persons. Without it, faith in God could not be purged; nor could it be anything other than the confidence of the gambler.

167. The above discussion has to do with the authority of God but similar remarks maybe made about the authority of Christ. The teaching of Jesus was with authority but it was not authoritarian, for he was gentle and lowly of heart (Matthew 11:29), and was amongst men and women as a servant (Mark 10:42-45). His words were made authoritative by his deeds, and by his life as a whole (John 5:36). Similarly, the modern believer, in submitting to the authority of Christ, does not capitulate to a Christ-centred credulity, but searches to know the spirit of Christ, for many 'false Christs' have come into the world (1 John 2:18). The authenticity of Christ is seen in the integrity (wholeness or consistency) of scripture (how significant it is for this problem that there are four Gospels and not just one!), of traditional doctrine, of Christian experience and so on. It is true in a way that one never leaves the circle. There is no greater love than the love of Christ by which the love of Christ could be seen to be true love. But it is a circle not a point. The dilation of the circle so that a pattern or a harmony of many elements can be perceived, so that one aspect may be seen against another, sets up an internal dialogue in faith and gives faith its living room, within which it acts self-critically, and does not become fanatical. The faith which is a gift of God is not blind, but, in the likeness of its Giver, it is full of eyes.

Summary: Either the divine authority is presented to us with reasons, in which case we must discern them in critical openness in order to obey God, or on the other hand, God is a dictator.

CRITICAL OPENNESS AND REVELATION

168. At first sight, the Christian idea of revelation might look ill at ease with the Christian idea of critical openness, for it might seem to exalt the reason of man against the revelation of God. But the calling to critical openness *flows from* the nature of the Christian revelation of God as being one who offers himself to man. It is *part* of the revelation and should not be thought of as being hostile to it. Only when God is thought of as being authoritarian and his self-revealing is thought of as being outside the context of personal life, an imposition external to the person, can critical openness be thought of as exalting the reason of man against the divine revelation. For if God is not authoritarian, then it must be that through his revelation of himself as being not authoritarian he is summoning us to critical openness. God, in willing to bring us to personhood, may adopt only such means as are compatible with personhood and which tend to the creation of persons. But autonomy or critical openness is an essential attribute of personhood. Authoritarianism and autonomy are incompabile. According to the criteria of personhood and what it entails, God is wise, wise in selecting this goal from the lesser goals which might have been selected, and wise in selecting the kinds of relation with his creatures which are best suited to the accomplishment of this goal. It is God's wise decree that his creatures should be critically open. God has called us into fellowship with himself, having made us mind as well as spirit. The fellowship of spirit with spirit is love and the fellowship of mind with mind is critical openness. The criteria for this situation are drawn from the nature of mind itself. Theism without critical openness (a dictatorial God) would empty the Christian view of man of its dignity, the rational soul, the image of God, and it would empty God of his role as the creator and saviour of persons.

169. The revelation of God is received supremely through Jesus Christ. He is described as the logos of God (John 1:1) without whom nothing was made. The logos is the light of men and becomes man. The life of critical openness which the believer lives is a fellowship with this one who is himself the expression of the universal coherence and harmony of God. But this life is a fellowship of like with ('conformed to the image of his Son'), (Romans 8:29) not a substitution of the logos for our human minds. The heteronomous believer follows an Apollinarian Christ, one whose mind is replaced by the logos of God. Some Christians misinterpreting such texts as 2 Cor. 10:5 and Gal. 2:20, seek to give up their minds, to have them replaced by the mind of God. But the mystery of Christian fellowship 'in Christ' is a mystery of 'walking with the Lord', being 'in communion' with him, not a situation where our human minds are invaded and expelled by God's mind. The same reasoning which led the church to reject the Apollinarian heresy leads to the life of critical openness, both in its response to Christ as the logos of God and in its imitation of Jesus, true man and true God.

170. Was Jesus critically open? His teaching about the incoming Kingdom indicates his openness towards the end of Judaism as he knew it. Jesus' secure love and faith enabled him to be critically open in ethics, towards the law and

so on. It is however a form of critical openness which leads to the courage to do rather than to what we would call autonomous speculation. Jesus operated beneath an umbrella of Jewish faith; he was not a critical theist of the Greek kind. Nevertheless, Jesus did realise and react to radical questions of his society, limited as all societies are by the prevailing world view. For our part, we must be as critical of our Western culture (including its Greek inheritance) as Jesus was of the history and institutions of Israel. So even although our context is wider than that of Jesus he has certainly manifested the ideal of Christian critical openness.

Summary: Far from being hostile to the idea of critical openness, the idea of Christian revelation leads the believer towards it, since God reveals himself in Christ as one who desires not dominion over slaves but fellowship with sons and daughters.

THE NATURE OF GOD

171. The idea of finality led us to consider authority and that in turn led us into a consideration of the nature of Christian revelation. But what of the God who is so revealed? We have spoken of him as seeking to promote personal life, as autonomy is a feature of personhood, seeking to advance autonomy. But God is person. Can God be thought of then as critically open? God is clearly autonomous. He thinks for himself seeing that he is supreme intelligence and knows everything. But can he be thought of as possessing those special features which made us prefer the expression 'critical openness' to 'autonomy'? *We* must be open because we know that our knowledge is only a fraction of the total sum of knowledge, and we must be critical because we so easily mistake falsehood for knowledge. But the divine knowledge is perfect in its quality and in its extent. God knows all there is to be known, and he knows it infallibly and in perfect accuracy of detail. Indeed he knows it as its Creator rather than, or as well as, its Observer. Add to all this the traditional assertion that God's knowledge, like his being, is eternal and 'eternally simultaneous', that the past and the future are as totally present to him as is the present. It seems then that in God there can be no learning, no surprise at the novelties which are thrown up in our expanding universe, even those novelties that come from the free decisions of other centres of consciousness and will, and so God can have no critical openness!

172. On the other hand, scripture licenses a different vocabulary for speaking of God. He remembers our sins no more, relents in his punishments, awaits us with loving-kindness, enters into resolutions befitting the turn of events, is involved in the progress of his people and delights in his creations. In fact it might be said that the God of scripture is critically open in all the ways in which we are – towards the future, towards the actions and needs of others, in selecting from present possibilties, in discriminating between values, but without the weaknesses in our criticism imposed upon us by the

fact that we are never acquainted with all the facts, and the limitations upon our openness imposed by the fact that we build barriers between ourselves and other creatures.

173. It will be said that this language is anthropomorphic. But the most 'metaphysical' of religious language itself retains anthropomorphic elements. (Language is not less anthropomorphic simply by being more abstract.) And it is surely wise, in moving from scriptural imagery of God to philosphical conceptualisation, to beware of straining too much in the quest for an unattainable purity. God's being is fuller, not thinner, than anything we can properly conceive and articulate. And if there are aspects or components of critical openness, as we have described it, that are attractive in themselves and not merely as means to further ends, that belong to the perfection of spirit and not only to its process, then must we not attribute them also to God, indeed as to their apotheosis? Are there such aspects or components of critical openness? There would seem to be two (related) essential ingredients of critical openness as an ideal, namely an attentive (loving) receptivity to the wondrous world that is in principle without limits (that puts no *priori* limits on itself) on the one hand, and on the other the will and the skill to distinguish the true from the merely plausible. But these would seem each to belong to the ideal perfection of the life of the spirit. If this is so, then they may be attributed to God. And, indeed, is it not enough to state them in this way to see that they do belong to God, and in supereminent manner? God is the One who is open and attentive, so lovingly attentive as never to be deceived, not fitfully and to but some creatures as we are, but eternally and to all creatures. We can even say of his critical openness (as of his knowledge and his love – of which in the end his critical openness is an essential aspect) that it *sustains* all being and all developments in being, that it therefore sustains also *our* critical openness, our aspiration to be perfect like our heavenly Father, in this respect also.

174. Man therefore in being critically open is, however imperfectly, in the image of God. The thought is perhaps a strange one, because the vocabulary is not the traditional religious vocabulary. But the appeal to be 'perfect as your Father in heaven is perfect' (Matt 5:48) if it means that we should be perfect in this respect and in that respect – whatever these maybe which are appropriate perfections for creatures to aspire towards – may be construed as including amongst these many respects this one: to be critically open (within the limits of finitude) as God is critically open (within the limits of infinitude). How are we to live before such a God? This brings us to the question of spirituality.

Summary: God himself maybe thought of as having that kind and degree of critical openness appropriate to his perfect nature. In living in critical openness we are imitators of him

SPIRITUALITY AND CRITICAL OPENNESS

175. People sometimes ask whether we are to be critically open at the

expense of our loyalty to Christ.The question arises because critical openness is not one of the traditional Christian virtues, but is preconceived as being in potential hostility to Christian commitment. Christians seldom ask whether we should be loving at the expense of our loyalty to Christ. To be loving is to be Christian. But, in a less important but still significant way, to be critically open is also to be Christian. Christians have no monopoly of love just as they have no monopoly of critical openness, but the logic of their faith drives them in these directions and gives a distinctive meaning to their love and their criticism. But traditional Christian spirituality with its emphasis on such virtues as obedience and submissiveness might seem ill at ease with a spirituality of critical openness. This feeling (for it is no more) arises simply because the implications of critical openness for spirituality are not thought through. So the following comments are offered.

176. Critical openness is sometimes thought of as if it exhibited a proud spirit instead of a mood of self-repudiating acceptance. This is usually a mistake. The critically open person cannot but be humble, because in his openness to others he acknowledges his need for help, and in his criticism he acknowledges his own fallibility. Inasmuch as critical openness is certainly not thinking what appeals to you or believing what you like or accepting what makes you comfortable (see para. 15), it is a repudiation of self-centredness. The critically open person is the one who knows he has much to learn. The critically open Christian is far removed from the one who has the 'spirit of fear' (Romans 8:15). Instead he exercises Christian responsibility, is a son not a slave, and seeks to test everything, in order to hold fast that which is good.

177. It is true that there is some New Testament imagery which might seem to emphasise the passivity and the dependence of discipleship. We are sheep, a little flock, branches of the vine, we are to leave all and to follow him without question or delay. But other strands emphasise Christian responsibility – we are to count the cost like the king setting out to war, we are to take risks with our talents, we are to be wise as serpents. Moreover, critical openness is part of the abandoning of the old securities which is part of discipleship. How could Jewish men who were not critically open have responded to the question of Jesus about who he was? It should also be pointed out that to belong to the school of Christ cannot be similar to belonging to the school of (say) Aristotle. The follower of Aristotle seeks to elaborate the system of Aristotle. But Jesus founded no system, wrote no book.

DOUBT

178. The criticism which flows from faith is not the only kind of questioning which the Christian may experience. There is also the problem of sinful doubt. In the New Testament we read not only of the testing which is required of the alert, expectant eschatolological church but also of those who deliberately or in blindness turn from the light, falling even deeper into their

sin (Mark 3:28f; John3:19-21; 8:43). How are we to distinguish between the scepticism to which faith is called by faith itself and the doubt which is the product of sin and leads to further sin?

179. The Christian must examine his own motives carefully. Is it the case that after years of calm confidence, I am now beginning to question Christian faith? Then could this be because I have become too comfortable? Is it because I am falling prey to intellectual arrogance? Is it through my laziness in allowing my faith to remain puerile while the rest of my thinking becomes more sophisticated? Is it because I am chafing under the sacrificial implications of Christian faith? Or it is, on the other hand, because my complacency is at last being shattered by the realisation that the Lord has yet more light and truth to break forth from his word? Is it that I am growing out of shallow and defensive dogmatism? Is it that my faith has until now been heteronomous but at last I am beginning to struggle with my personal vocation to become mature in Christ? The thoughtful Christian will acknowledge that his criticism is itself part of his life which must be tested by the same enquiring spirit. The false prophets and the true are not only found in the world outside. They are also in our own hearts. But clearly it can be no answer to play safe, to refuse the calling of mature criticism because of a fear of falling into sinful doubt. The servant who did not dare take any risk, but hid his talent in the ground, was condemned by his master for being too scrupulous, when he knew all the time that his master was very demanding. And, although the reality of sinful doubt must never be minimised, the doctrine of justification by faith may give us some encouragement and release us from the inhibiting fears of doubt, which might otherwise paralyse Christian criticism.

JUSTIFICATION BY FAITH

180. It may be that critical openness cannot be made compatible with the Presbyterian doctrine of the covenant, as it developed in seventeenth century Protestant scholasticism, in which the idea that the covenant is bestowed conditionally creates a series of limits, which, if transgressed, place one outside the covenant. But if the older reformed principle of justification by faith is taken seriously, and extended into the intellectual realm as well as the moral realm, then the Christian, being accepted regardless of conditions, is set free from intellectually inhibiting religious fears. There are no degrees of justification. The justified Christian is thus set free from fear in order to pursue God's path to personhood. Just as in ethics, justification by faith sets the Christian free to respond to new situations, so critical openness is the life of the Christian mind, flowing from the same principle – which itself is open to critical reflection, and so on forever. We can see therefore that critical openness is *not* a basic Christian concept (such as the grace of God is) but a derived or consequential attribute of Christian living. It is derived from ideas such as the personhood of God, the nature of

66

the divine image, the Christian hope in the future, the character of discipleship towards Jesus and so on, and we are emboldened to walk this way because of justification by faith. The old Christian symbol of this is not the maze, which presents one with many hazardous choices, but the single-track labyrinth. This is an incredibly convoluted path, with innumerable doublings back, apparent lack of progress, a sudden coming near the goal only to be thrust out to the perimeter, and yet away in which, at the last, there is no being lost.

181. Is lack of critical openness culpable for the modern Christian? The pluralistic situation of modern Western society is without precedent. Whether this will be a lasting condition of the West we do not know. But clearly in this situation, as long as it lasts, it is most important for the future of Christian faith that it should be critically open both towards itself and towards its fellow (or rival) world views. If we are in a melting-pot stage, in which the outlines of a new synthesis are being forged (*i.e.* when pluralism will be overcome in some new kind of society) then it is even more vital for Christians, by exercising critical openness, to play an active part in the shaping of this. We conclude that it would be culpable for the church to neglect this, and that, to some extent, in ways appropriate to his or her other gifts and callings, each Christian should endeavour to make some contribution to Christian critical openness.

Summary: Christian critical openness is consistent with a loving, trusting, responsible spirituality. It may be distinguished from the doubt which springs from sin, and the Christian is encouraged in criticism by his justification by faith. Critical openness is a calling to which all Christians in pluralist societies must respond.

CRITICAL OPENNESS AS A DISCIPLINE

182. Christian critical openness is thus a discipline which the Christian follows not in spite of his faith but because of it. But there is no question here of Christian theology being reduced to meet the requirements of the dialogue with secular education, or the needs of Christian nurture in a plural society. Rather, we are trying to listen to Christian faith itself, in order to hear whether it does indeed offer resources for this task. We have not tried to adapt Christian faith to a secular idea of autonomy, but we have tried to establish a Christian ideal of critical openness, witnessed to by the New Testament and demanded by the nature of Christian faith.

LIMITS TO CRITICAL OPENNESS

183. But are there limits to Christian critical openness? To limit criticism would be to resist learning and so declare that development was complete.

But what if criticism were to indicate that all the sacred relics were forgeries, the gospels without historical foundation and their concept of God incoherent? What if criticism explodes the Christian faith? This possibility expresses the ambiguity of faith and it cannot be removed, either by criticism itself or by naive assertion. To restrain criticism because it seemed to be going in the wrong direction would be such an act of intellectual dishonesty that the ethics of Christian intellectual life would be destroyed in any case. After all, if criticism were justified in dissolving faith one would be left with something more closely approaching the truth than one had before, whereas if criticism were restrained because of fear of unwelcome conclusions, one would be left with neither the best truth available nor the Christian faith (since its intellectual calling would have been betrayed).

184. It should be understood that the idea of there being no limits to Christian critical openness is a methodological principle. It is because it is to do with method that Christian critical openness can recoil upon the axioms out of which it springs (*e.g.* it springs from faith in a certain kind of God, yet it can also ask if there is such a God). The *content* of Christian faith pushes us towards the *method* of critical openness, and the content cannot be immune from the method it dictates, even although we do not know what method might be dictated by any content of faith which might follow the present content if that were to be destroyed by criticism. In emphasising that this is a method, we mean that the Christian must act *as if* it were *possibly* the case that his beliefs were false. An alarmist reaction would be quite inappropriate – we do not actually think that Christian faith is anywhere near the point of collapse, but we must accept the possibility if our intellectual quest is to have integrity. The paradigm under which the Christian quest is conducted must itself be questioned, and indeed, it invites us to question it. This can be seen in Jesus' questions, 'Why do you call me good?' 'Whom do men say that I am?' 'Having ears, do you hear?' Note that a similar methodological readiness for doubt is required from the atheist. This is a method of enquiry, to which the Christian is prompted by special reasons of his own, but which is also mandatory for all thinking and testing of hypotheses.

185. The other side of methodological sceptism is methodological dogmatism. Without dogmatism there could be no critical openness, for rigorous and searching enquiry would be impossible if beliefs were abandoned at the first breath of doubt. It is only the beliefs which are cared about enough to struggle over, to commit oneself to, to defend to the end, which can receive the deepest criticism. This is as true in the case of scientific research as it is of theology. But this element of dogmatism is important because it creates the conditions for critical openness, not because it limits its scope. Dogmatism without criticism is sterile, and criticism wihout dogmatism is empty.

Summary: Christian critical openness is not only a theology and a spirituality but also a method of enquiry. Although in principle it has no limits it must be balanced by a certain element of dogmatism without which the criticism itself would seldom be sufficiently sustained and penetrating.

Chapter 10

CHRISTIAN NURTURE AND RELIGIOUS EDUCATION

186. We have seen that Christian nurture is similar to secular education in that both are committed to enquiry, both are concerned with learning in order to make yet further learning possible. By virtue of this characteristic, Christian faith may provide a rationale for both kinds of processes, since Christian faith is driven towards this position by its own internal logic. We can therefore speak of 'Christian education' in the sense of a Christian rationale for the processes of learning, and of 'Christian nurture' in the sense of a Christian rationale (and in this case there could be no other kind of rationale) for a Christian learning about Christian faith leading to deeper Christian faith. Christian nurture can thus be defended against the charge that it is closed authoritarian instruction, and its humane and ethical status are assured.

187. But does our discussion prove too much? We began with the problem of how Christian nurture could possess critical openness and yet intend the deepening of Christian faith. We saw that education and Christian nurture each share in the spirit of enquiry. Have we now reached a point where the similarity between Christian nurture and general education is so close that any thing a child might gain from Christian nurture he could in any case have gained from his education, *i.e.* a county school religious education including Christian Studies? Is there any particular benefit to be gained from Christian nurture?

COMMITMENT AND CRITICAL OPENNESS

188. First we should remember the differing hopes or intentions of the Christian nurturer and the educator teaching Christian Studies (see para. 145). Christian nurture, through its critical openness, can contemplate the possibilities of the collapse of Christian faith, but what it expects, hopes for and intends is the strengthening of Christian faith. Critical openness tests, expands and fulfils Christian faith. Christian nurture is based upon the hypothesis that Christianity is true and can be seen to be yet more true. There is nothing odd or illogical about the combination of this commitment with this critical openness. Scientific commitment and enquiry have similar features. We have already noted (para. 185) the place of dogmatism in science, pointing out that only if the adherents of theories defend them vigorously, try by every scientific means to secure them against attack, try to adapt them to meet objections, and set high standards for their overthrow, can science be protected from the situation where theories were lightly advanced and easily given up. The commitment ensures the depth of probing without which the

advance of truth would be difficult because the discussion would be superficial. In religion, although the word 'dogmatism' is best avoided because of its pejorative history, the same is true. It is only sensible that there should be a *strong* commitment to rational religious beliefs provided they are held in the spirit of critical openness and with the contemplation of the possibility (although not the expectation of the likelihood) that they may be false. In the case of the Christian religion, where the commitment and the criticism flow from the same central ideas, the connection is still more evident and coherent.

FAITH, NURTURE AND EDUCATION

189. Secondly, we should remember the relation between Christian theology and education and nurture respectively. It has already been pointed out (para. 145) that there can be no other rationale for Christian nurture than that provided by Christian theology, which is therefore in a necessary and sufficient relationship to the practice of Christian nurture. But Christian theology has but a partial and a possible relation to the practice of education.

190. Combining these two distinctions, we may say that Christian nurture is a servant of faith, and it is this faithful service which impels it to be critically open towards faith itself, as faith in the Christian sense requires, but education, although also *capable* of being justified by faith, is an independent activity of secular man. Reversing the servant metaphor, we may say that theology is lord of Christian nurture (Christian nurture is captive to theology (see para. 181)) but theology is servant to education. Theology appraises education, tries to illumine, but cannot prescribe, except in circumstances when education, becomes itself captive to ideologies hostile to Christian faith, and then education is no longer open to being compatible with Christian education, and Christian theology must denounce it. But as long as a Christian rationale for secular education is *possible,* that interpretation remains as a service. There can be necessary attack (where education has become anti-Christian) but there can be no *necessary* support, because non-Christians can be educators. This question has to do with the circumstances when the saying 'He that is not against us is for us' (Mark 9:40) must be exchanged for the saying 'He who is not with me is against me, and he who does not gather with me scatters' (Luke 11:23). The critical openness of Christian nurture is a Christian critical openness; the critical openness of education is merely compatible with Christian faith.

191. The third reason for maintaining the education/Christian nurture distinction has to do with the spheres in which the two activities take place, or their social agencies. Christian nurture is a domestic activity of the church; education is a public activity of the state, assuming that in certain circumstances the state has the right to educate, although like all other rights of the state, there are limits to its operation.

70

192. The fourth reason why Christian nurture is different from education has to do with the pedagogical character of the two processes, but is also connected with the nature of the agencies or spheres. In principal (*e.g.* in certain countries of Asia) a satisfactory religious education need make but minor reference to Christianity. And even in western countries, pupils can become educated concerning several or any religions. But because it is prolongation of the conditions of infancy, a prolongation which seeks to bring the infant to maturity and not keep him in infancy, and yet begins from the conditions of infancy and takes them seriously as the inheritance of the child, a child can *only* be nurtured in his own religion. You can indoctrinate a child into anything, and in the case of Christianity, that would mean alienating him from his Christian family tradition, and you can educate a child into anything worthwhile, and in the case of Christianity, that would mean respecting but not necessarily promoting his Christian family tradition.

193. The fifth mark of Christian nurture as against education is that Christian nurture proceeds from an assumption that teacher and learner are *inside* the Christian faith (see Appendix I), whereas education only invites the pupil to *imagine* what it would be like to be inside a faith, or (in the situation where a pupil is being educated in his own faith) education invites the pupil to imagine what it would be like to be *outside* his faith. The whole environment of the secular school, the plurity present in the classroom, the range of teacher commitments, the nature and style of the public examinations – all contribute to this ethos. Suspension of belief or disbelief is an important part of educational method in the religious area, but has a smaller and different role to play in Christian nurture.

194. The sixth distinction is that education in religion is appropriate for all, but Christian nurture is appropriate only for Christians. Christian nurture is based upon the belief that there are Christian children (see Chapter 11). Finally, Christian nurture takes place in the context of worship, in a specialised faith community, where the child, as a Christian, learns from the Word of God (see Chapter 15). These factors give Christian nurture an ethos, an emotional context, which are quite different from that provided by education in county schools.

195. Of course it may be the case that these distinctions make little practical difference in some situations, especially with adolescent pupils. It may be that even young people within the churches are so deeply secularised that with them as the general pupils in the state schools all that the teacher, whether Christian nurturer or religious educator, can offer is a fundamental pre-catechesis or introduction which will begin to make learning possible in these areas. But even where this were the case, and the starting point was thus similar, the ending point would be different. As the processes got under way, the differences would emerge, or, if they did not, the teacher might have succeeded as educator whilst his colleague in the church might have failed as Christian nurturer.

Summary: Although Christian nurture shares critical openness with secular education, there is still much that is distinctive about Christian nurture. Its setting within a worshipping community of faith and its deliberate intention to promote faith enable the Christian child to find in Christian nurture what he cannot find from his religious education in a county school.

CHILDREN ARE CRITICALLY OPEN

196. Critical openness is a childlike quality. It was the child who pointed out that the Emperor had no clothes. In the novels of George MacDonald, C.S. Lewis and many others, it is children who through their curiosity, love of adventure and readiness for a 'change of world' are able to enter the enchanted kingdom while the adults for the most part remain sceptical, indifferent, busy or ignorant. A baby explores his world with unbounded zest for new experiences – a crackly piece of paper, a furry coat, a bowl of water will attract his playing fingers and his probing mind. It is a mark of greatness to retain critical openness with advancing years. For most adults, capacity for new learning decreases with increasing age, and we tend as we grow older to be more content with what we know already. It was the Little Prince who had the insight, the hobbits who set out on the perilous quest. It is because the Kingdom of God is available to those who knock, seek, and ask, and are receptive enough to what may be on the other side of the door, that children are not only suitable for life in the Kingdom but typical members of it (Mark 10:14). Training in critical openness is thus not to be thought of as being best suited for adult education in the churches, or to be confined to young people. It is equally if not more suitable for the youngest child.

197. It might be thought that the word 'nurture' suggests a careful protective nourishment, a guarding from possible dangers, perhaps even a seclusion from danger (see para. 132). This can hardly be the case with the process of Christian upbringing which we are describing, or if it is so, then what the child needs to be guarded from is that his spirit of enquiry and free curiosity will be stunted. The approach we suggest is child-centred in that it intends to foster these attributes of children and young people, which are also attributes of the Kingdom and of the Christian faith into which they are growing. But it is not child-centred in that the child is not left in a vacuum. The openness is not emptiness; the criticism is exercised upon a rich world of knowledge and experience which is presented to him. This spirit of growth emerges from Christian faith and aspires to its fullness. It is from faith to faith. Therefore the child is to grow up in the Christian story, shaped by the overarching Christian *mythos,* surrounded by words, music and prayers of the community which is on the Way. So the approach we suggest is rich in implications for a Christian curriculum (see Appendix II)*. It is *because of* that Christian curriculum that he will find the skills and the freedom to exercise his critical openness *upon* that Christian curriculum.

THE DEMANDS ON ADULTS

198. It is not difficult to imagine the circumstances in which Christian children might be nurtured in such a Way, although it is much more difficult, since we are adults, to provide those circumstances. We have already mentioned the first such circumstance: the child must not be left merely to enjoy himself, merely to be happy, merely to have good relationships, but must encounter the strangeness, the wonder and the challenging power of the Christian tradition, especially in the Bible, from his earliest days. He cannot learn to speak unless he hears speech. He cannot think unless he has experiences to think about. Intellectual and emotional stimulation are thus of the greatest importance, and dullness, monotony and boredom the greatest enemies. Too much of the work with children in church is mere 'busy' work. It is not enough to copy out texts and draw pictures and make models, unless the child learns the Christian language that goes with the symbols. His mind must be engaged as well as his hands, and this is as important, at his own level of response, for the slower and less able as it is for the more able child.

199 Inasmuch as one cannot safely predict what will engage the interest of the child, or as what moment he will ask a delightful question, much of the work with children as well as with young people will be spontaneous. But because the teacher must try to precipitate these situations, be ready to recognise them, and know how to respond to a sudden flash of insight by showing that it is a facet of a still larger insight, it requires a high degree of preparation by teachers and parents. There must be continuity of experience from week to week and the experience of each given day (*e.g.* on a Sunday morning) must be consistent and harmonious. The child must perceive regularities (*e.g.* the same person appearing in a different story, the same symbol cropping up in a different context) but regularities are perceived in a setting variety. Without variety, regularity is not noticed. It becomes routine. This is not the place to pursue the implications of this kind of Christian nurture for curriculum and method (see Appendix II), but some of the questions moral in a conventional 'good boy' manner? Does the material used offer a one-dimensional appraoch to the Bible, in that no discrimination or variety of interpretation is attempted? Is the material and the activities 'busy' rather than challenging and reflective? Are new ideas, new words, new symbols introduced each week? Is there a deadening and inhibiting stress upon authority and obedience to God rather than upon response to God and sharing his creativity? Are facts presented without meanings? Is a range and diversity of patterns of Christian music, spirituality, kinds of worship and even ethical approaches presented, appropriate to the children's readiness?

200. Such Christian nurture can only be provided by Christian adults who are free and creative in their own religious thinking and living (see paras. 132 and 150). Preparation for such teaching will be devotionalism which takes the form of 'problematisation'. This is particularly important in the case of adult education and the training of parents. The difficulties, conflicts and dilemmas of Christian faith and life must be exposed for Christian adults, because the

problems are there anyway, and there can be no growth unless they are confronted.

Summary: Critical openness is for children, and ways can be found whereby Christian children as well as adults can be nurtured from and into this spirituality.

Chapter 11

CHRISTIAN CHILDHOOD

201. While Christian evangelism and even Christian instruction may be offered to those whose religious affiliation is uncertain, or who are clearly not Christians, Christian nurture, since this refers to the process of fostering or developing a state which already exists, can only be offered to Christians. But if children cannot be Christians, they cannot be the objects of Christian nurture. If the child cannot be thought of as being a Christian in any real and significant way, neither can he be thought of as being in the church in any real and significant way. In this case, the church's treatment of the child will be substantially different, or ought to be. The child can be evangelised. Of course, most of those who evangelise children believe that as a result of their response children can become Christians, but we are concerned with the question as to whether a child can be a Christian from baptism, or from birth, or in some way so as to mean that he is *in* the church and can be Christianly nurtured from his parents' knees.

202. Other thoughtful Christian adults do not think it advisable to evangelise children, especially younger and more impressionable ones. For those who take this view, and do not look upon children as already being Christians, the only remaining way to cause children to learn is by educating them. If a child cannot be a Christian except through evangelisation and if evangelisation is not for children, then there is nothing but education left. But in that case, there is no theological difference between the church's 'own' children (by whatever title they are described) and the children of good and noble traditions such as Islam and Humanism. In paragraphs 186 to 195 we have seen that Christian nurture has certain distinct features which general education in religion does not have, and on the supposition that only education can be suitable for children, these benefits would be denied to them. For example, the religious education of the county schools ought not to suppose that the child will participate in worship, prayer and sacraments. These are Christian nurturing activities only appropriate within the Christian church.

203. Finally in this opening discussion of the question, we note that if there can be no Christian children then there can be no Christian families. There can be Christian married couples and Christian adults sharing a common home, but there can be no Christian families. It is easy to see that the denial of the possibility of Christian childhood leads us directly into a sharply individualistic conception of the church and of society.

CAN CHILDREN BE CHRISTIANS ?

204. Discussions amongst theologians as to whether children can be considered Christians are similar to discussions amongst philosophers as to whether children can be considered to be persons. The question is whether

the child meets the criteria of personhood/Christian life. The criteria, although of course not identical, have enough in common for us to say with some confidence that for those who think a child cannot be a Christian, the child cannot be a person either.

205. So the question about the child in the church is first a question about the church. When the church is thought of as a corporate body (as, for example, in the autocephalous churches of Orthodoxy, to a lesser extent the national churches of Scandanavia and England/Scotland, or in societies with 'tribal' forms of association) then the child will be a member. But if a church emphasises individuality, egalitarianism, democracy, rights of conscience, idea of an educated person, rationality, private judgment, and thinks of itself as a fellowship, a society of believers, even an association or society, then the place of the child becomes doubtful, because he does not meet these criteria. When the criterion is that one is a member of a family, the child meets that as well as the adult, maybe better. Sacramental views are often important in this respect. The more sacramental, then the more communal, then the more natural the place of the child. The more inward, intellectual, 'fellowshippy' or verbal, the more doubtful the place of the child. Compare the unambiguous place the child has in Orthodoxy with the slight uncertainty in Anglicanism, the 'neither fish nor fowl' view of Methodism and Congregationalism (NB. the notion of 'junior' membership or the cradle roll) or with the question mark against the child in the Baptist tradition.

206. Of course, it may well be that in the present state of sociological levelling there is little or no practical difference in the way these churches treat their children, which partly raises the problem of the relationship in theology between theory and practice, and partly concerns the degree to which elements present in older forms of the tradition, when they were self conscious about each other, are simply no longer distinguishable. However these notions still seem to have some influence by way of the unquestioned assumptions of church life. Completely untutored Presbyterians are surprised by the thought that a child might be a church member. Completely untutored members of the Greek Orthodox Church are equally surprised at the thought that the child might not be. Doctrines when not purified by critical openness become assumptions.

207. At this point there is a difficulty common to all ecumenical dialogue. If questions of denominational tradition are clarified, there is a danger than a certain emphasis is seen as 'alien to our tradition'. But if they are ignored, then the deeper and often unconscious springs which guide the behaviour of church people (particularly in an activity such as the rearing of Christian children) remain untouched. The child is not to be denied his past, and this includes his past in previous centuries of the theology of childhood which his denomination has expressed. The importance of this in rethinking the place of the child in the church of today is underlined by the fact that a large proportion of Christian people go to churches other than the one in which they were reared themselves. We have therefore this strange mingling of assumptions which is both part of the problem and part of the answer.

208. The history of the nineteenth century Sunday School movement shows that the problems of the child in the church were somehow evaded by the creation of a 'para-church' structure (ie the Sunday School) which, notwithstanding the different denominational understandings of childhood, was pretty much the same in all the churches, because it was created by common sociological pressures and the common educational needs of society, and held together by evangelistic aims common to the churches. Now that this para-church is, on the whole, disappearing, the problem of the meaning of the life of the child, in the church emerges into the light of Christian consciousness. Whereas the nineteenth century church solved the problem by reacting to externals, leaving the liturgy and sacraments secure and untouched, we today must try to think *from the inside* about the Christian significance of the church child.

Summary: the process of Christian nurture depends upon the validity of the idea that a child can be a Christian and hence a member of the church from his earliest days. The Christian denominations have various traditions concerning the place and estimation of childhood. These must be explored in order to enable us to formulate a policy for today.

THE BIBLE AND CHRISTIAN CHILDHOOD

209. The biblical basis for Christian childhood is rather stronger than it is for infant baptism, since the arguments for the latter often depend upon inference or even silence. Christian childhood is a somewhat more general concept than baptised childhood, and more general evidence will be relevant. But we wish to emphasise that we are not immediately concerned with the sacramental question. Most of the modern discussions about infant baptisms have been motivated by a concern for the meaning of baptism rather than for the meaning of childhood in the church.

210. The child had an accepted place in Israel. The children were present at the passover meal, and took an active part in the ritual (Exodus 12:26). Children were with in the covenant and received circumcision as a sign of their participation in the relation with God (Genesis 17:7). Several prophets were regarded as sacred from their birth (1 Samuel 1:11; Judges 13:5; Luke 1:15) and began their ministries in childhood (1 Samuel 2 and 3) or were full of the Holy Spirit from or before birth (Luke 1:15).

211. The teaching of Jesus is clear on the point, provided we do not expect to find direct references to expressions such as 'being Christian'. The child 'in the midst' is the representative of Christ and of God (Mark 9:36f) and the little ones believe in Christ (Mark 9:42). Children receive the blessing of Christ who describes them as not only belonging to the Kingdom (or rather, the Kingdom belongs to them) but adds that the Kingdom can only be received as a child (Mark 10:14-16). In Matthew's account (18:3) repentance, necessary in order to enter the Kingdom, is associated with becoming a child.

This verse alone would be sufficient for us to ask not whether a child can be a Christian but whether an adult can. The various references to family churches and family baptism in the Acts and Letters although perhaps inconclusive for infant baptism are surely quite convincing on the more general point of child membership in the church and their status as Christians. Paul speaks of the faith which had been in Timothy's grandmother and his mother and is now in him (2 Timothy 1:5;) who from childhood had known the scriptures (2 Timothy 3:15).

212. The childhood of Jesus himself is important for this question. When Paul tells children to obey their parents in everything (Colossians 3:20), adding 'for this pleases the Lord' we may well be reminded of the obedience of the child Jesus to his own parents (Luke 2:51). His infancy is venerated (Matthew 2:11) and we have no reason to exclude his childhood from the general instructions to imitate Christ. The infant John the Baptist may be regarded as the first who responded to the infant Christ – a favourite subject of medieval art – hearing the voice of Mary and leaping in his mother's womb (Luke 1:41 and 44). The expression 'in the Lord' which is used by Paul to describe the relation of the Christian to Christ is used of children, who are to obey their parents 'in the Lord' (Ephesians 6:1) and it is continually 'in the Lord' that their upbringing is to take place (Ephesians 6:4). The very fact that children are addressed in the ethical sections of the letters along with fathers, mothers, masters and slaves shows that the children were thought of as an accepted part of the church, subject to its discipline, incorporated within it, not as 'junior members' but as sharing fully in the life of the congregation. There seems little doubt then that the teaching and practice of both Jesus and the early church was such that the church received children into its midst, and that this is the origin of the church's practice which continued until the individualism of the Renaissance and the Reformation created the modern ambituity, which is mainly confined to Protestantism.

Summary: The practice of ancient Israel, the teaching and practice of Jesus, as well as his own childhood, and the custom and teaching of the early church are unanimous in the belief that children may be members of the church as fellow Christians, sharing with adults the life of the spirit and being 'in Christ'.

CHRISTIANS ARE CALLED

213. Having looked briefly at some of the biblical precedent and argument about the child as a Christian, let us consider another line of thought. Christian existence is summoned into life by God. If we are to take the description which Christianity offers of itself as a serious source for our understanding of what it means to be a Christian or who can become one, we must begin not with distinguishing marks or minimum qualifications or problems of criteria, but with the idea that being a Christian is a calling, a vocation. Before it is a response, it is a call. Christian faith understands itself not in the first place as a club, a society, an organisation, a tradition, but firstly as springing from a

reality, God, who remains the initiator of faith in himself.

214. We do not know for sure or in detail the extent or the limits of the divine calling. It may be, for example, that all mankind is called by God, and if this is so, then in a sense all souls may be thought of as Christian souls. From this perspective, Muslims may be considered Christians if they are hearing and responding to the divine call. In the same way, Christians may be thought of Muslims if they do indeed submit to God. Abraham is regarded as the first Jew. But Paul regards him as the founder of faith (*i.e.* Christian faith) and in the Qur'an he is the first Muslim. In such cases, the logic of the theological category ('Christian', 'Muslim') is wider than the actual limits of the empirical religious tradition which carries it. But that does not mean that this use of the theological idea is illogical. So in this broadest of all senses of the word Christian, we may not *begin* by denying than any individual, group, class or people is Christian. We *begin* with the thought of the *possibility* that the person or group *may* be Christian.

215. When we come to consider particular cases, whether of individuals or classes, we may find reason for concluding that the possibility is actually a *probability* (St Peter) or an *improbability* (Adolf Hitler) but as long as we confine ourselves strictly to Christian self-understanding (*i.e.* the account of being a Christian offered by Christianity) we never move from the view that it is extremely unlikely to the view that it is *impossible*. So far our discussion shows us that with children as a class and with individual children we can never assert an impossibility that they are Christians. There may be circumstances in which this possibility may become a greater or lesser degree of probability.

THE COVENANT OF GRACE AND THE CHILD

216. What theological circumstances might turn the general possibility of a child being a Christian into a probability? We began by insisting on the divine prerogative. Continuing the same line of thought, we may ask whether, in faith, we have grounds for thinking that the calling of God might be extended in some special ways to some. Christian faith affirms that this is indeed the case. God does not withold himself from any, but at least as an intermediate stage in calling all, he specially calls some, or he specially calls some as a step to calling all (Genesis 12:1-3). It is traditional in Protestant thought to describe these special stages or kinds of callings as covenants. A covenant is God's offering of himself in certain specified ways to all or some people. So the possibility of a general calling by God of all human beings would be a general covenant. The giving of himself as a God who establishes a regular course of nature might be thought of as such a general covenant. There are, according to biblical thought, also covenants which extend from the particular (Abraham) to the general (all nations). Such a particular self-giving took place, according to Christian faith, in the relation between God and Israel. This is not to deny that other equally particular relations did *not*

also exist between God and other peoples. It is only a point out that faith claims, on the basis of a particular historical experience, that God *has* given himself in *this* way to *these* people.

217. But children are specifically included within this sphere of this particular self-giving. At least, some children *are;* we are not told that other children are *not.* We have seen that this was the case both with the covenant with Abraham, which was with him and his children, and in Jesus' conception of the Kingdom of God, of which the Church is the symbol. So if a child stands within the sphere of this particular self-giving of God, the probability that he is a Christian increases. There is also a probability that he might be a Jew, but we are trying not to think according to the history or description of religions but only from within the logic of the Christian faith's own understanding of itself. But the probability, in the case of children of whom nothing more than this can be said, remains a slight one. For there were false children who rebelled, children who did not acknowledge their father and so on. So what theological circumstances might heighten the probability a little more? What are the indications that a person actually does stand within the sphere of this self-giving of God through Christ to the church?

218. To 'stand within the sphere' is partly a matter of hearing (Romans 10:14-21). One stands within this relationship if one is addressed by its terms and conditions, if one is spoken to by its symbols. In a wider sense, this encompasses every person to whom the message of God in Christ has been presented but it applies more exactly to those who are continually addressed, whose whole lives are lived under the call of the symbols, whose history carries with it this calling, whose personhood, received as gift, already contains the marks of this covenanted relationship. But this is the case of young children of Christian parents active in the church who grow up within the sphere and the daily influence of the Gospel.

INFANT BAPTISM

219. In acknowledging, expressing and confirming this reality, most churches baptise infants, even babies. This however does not mean that unbaptised children are *not* Christians. They may show other signs of standing within the sphere or they may be called of God even although we can see *no* signs. Some Christian groups in the past held the view that if a child died in infancy that in itself was a sign that the infant stood in covenant relation to God even although no previous signs of grace had been visible. They argued that it would be incredible that such an infant dying soon after birth should not be recieved by a loving God. However strange the need for such an argument may seem to most modern Christians, it is a reminder of the generally tolerant attitude towards the question of Christian childhood which, whether expressed in this form or some different theology, has been a feature of Christian faith. So although we must insist that the argument carries with it

no harshly negative conclusions concerning other children, it is clear that as far as *these* children are concerned, their parents on behalf of the believing community and the community on behalf of the parents, *intend* to address the child, and believe that the child, because of the theological circumstances which surrouind his birth and infancy, has a right to be so addressed. Moreover, this addressing and sealing under the name of Jesus Christ will normally be followed by a sustained process of further hearing and responding. If then, at that stage, the child by his own character, habits, outlook and interests, deepens the sense in which he appears to stand within the sphere of God's gracious covenant, then the faith of the church which baptised him will be confirmed and the probability that this is a Christian child will be still further enhanced.

Summary: Being a Christian is a matter of a particular kind of divine initiative and there are plenty of cases where the church has every reason to believe that this divine initiative has been exercised towards infants and children. Since the signs of this initiative are evident we have no reason to deny the name of 'Christian' to such children.

SACRAMENTAL INCORPORATION AND THE CHILD

220. The discussion in the previous section was based on a version of the traditional Protestant Reformed idea of the child in the covenant of grace. It forms part of the heritage of the Church of Scotland, the United Reformed Church, the Church of England and several smaller churches. It has a certain fitness here, because the calling to critical openness and the calling to covenanted commitment are two sides of the one coin. But the Christian nurture of children today must take place in an ecumenical context, and we have absolutely no intention to emphasise denominational peculiarities. There are several ways in which Christian childhood may be understood. The urgent need is for the churches to rediscover and recreate these, so that once again we might have a coherent rationale for Christian up-bringing adapted for the conditions of modern society and the ecumenical church of today.

221. Fortunately for the Christian nurture of Christian children, the largest churches *not* clearly linked or not associated at all the theological of the covenanted child adopt a theology which guarantees the place of the Christian child even more firmly. The Orthodox and Roman Catholic theologies have generally emphasised that the child is incorporated into the church sacramentally. Whereas in the Reformed tradition the child is *baptised* because he is a Christian (probably!) the other view, which includes important parts of the Anglican tradition as well, is that the child baptised in order *to make* him a Christian. In the former case, faith is in the promise. In the latter case, faith is in the sacrament, or rather, the promise is seen as fulfilled in the grace of the sacrament. This remains so even though in contemporary Catholic theology, which is reflected in the revised Catholic rite of baptism, more stress than previously is laid on the roles of the family

and the gathered assembly as the instruments of the infant's *ongoing* Christian vocation.

222. Now, the grace of the promise is always hidden to some extent within the mystery of the divine calling. But the grace of the sacrament is open and evident to all. According to the Reformed tradition, it would be uncharitable but not illogical to doubt that these children were indeed children of promise. The real children of promise, known only to God, *might* after all be some other children. But this supposition, although consistent with the Reformed doctrine of election, would be unloving towards the actual children in the church. For the Anglican, Catholic and Orthodox traditions, the possiblity that these children are not Christian, although baptised according to the faith and order of the church, would be more like an illogicality, since the supposition would run directly counter to the theology. This is why childhood has such an assured place within these churches, the Catholic church for example having elaborated the sacramental view of childhood into a whole series of sacramental steps, each one related to the needs of a different stage of development and forming a sort of liturgical and psychological stage theory of Christian growth. For the Church of England, where the question of infant baptism (in contrast with some Free Churches) has been not so much whether or not to baptise any but whether or not to baptise all, questions of the significance of Christian childhood have tended to gather round confirmation, as the fulfilment of the grace of baptism.

THE EMPHASIS ON RESPONSE AND PROFESSION OF FAITH

223. When we turn from the churches which may be thought of as emphasising *reception* of God's grace to those which lay stress upon *responding* or laying hold of God's grace, we find a different situation for Christian childhood. The imagery is found already within the Synoptic Gospels: it is as *children* that we *receive* the Kingdom, but it is as violent *men* that we *take* it by force (Matt. 11:12). The child is recipient is easily envisaged; it is less easy to identify the younger child as respondent. So whether the response is thought of in terms of 'assurance' or 'holiness' as in Methodism and the Salvation Army or as repentance and conversion as in the Baptist chruches (it is not being suggested that Methodists do not believe in conversion nor Baptists in holiness) the place of the child becomes less clear. With Congregationalism of the older type it was more a matter of the individualism associated with the idea of the gathered church which led to a similar emphasis upon responsibility. One *joined* such churches. They had membership registers, and although the corporate sense of identify might be extremely strong, they tended to think of themselves as societies (the Friends and the early Methodists).

224. In the older Free Churches the influence of Puritanism tended to discourage too much emphasis upon the sacraments, and this was an additional factor which led to infant baptism being less meaningful than in the

Catholic and Orthodox churches. Although infant baptism was still practised, especially in the Presbyterian churches, where the theology of the convenant continued to have influence, in many of the Free churches it become a rather mystifying ritual, since it was followed in adolescence by 'membership classes' and finally by reception into 'full' membership. The problem of the status of children who had been baptised was met by the creation of the 'cradle roll' or the idea of 'junior membership', although the idea of child membership seems often to have been little more than an analogy. The baptism service was often not very different from the child dedication services held by some Baptists, except for the use of the triune name and the water. But psychologically, in the minds of many parents, it has been little more than child dedication.

Summary: Views of children in the churches today reflect various strands, both covenanted and sacramental, or traditional denominational theologies.

The Plagues - Joseph Sinclair 6 yrs

84

Chapter 12

TRADITIONAL VIEWS OF CHILDHOOD IN THE CHURCHES

225. Let us examine a little more closely some of these traditional views of the significance of childhood in the churches. The theologies of childhood emerged during the formative periods of the history of denominations. These hidden doctines should be resurrected, not necessarily to be reaffirmed, but to be re-examined in the light of the theology of Christian nurture and critical openness. Perhaps if our modern understanding of Christian nurture is allowed to encounter the traditional theologies of childhood, a further step will have been taken towards a coherent policy. The main issues which the traditional theologies present are (i) the nature of the church, (ii) the meaning of baptism, (iii) the status of those to be baptised, (iv) the relation of infants to God and to the church.

226. The Roman Catholic and Orthodix views, although differing on certain questions (such as the administration of communion to infants) agree about child membership, baptismal incorporation and infant salvation. Both churches express, as we have seen, a view in which childhood is addressed by God through the sacraments, of which the church is the administrator.

227. Amongst the various evangelical groups, including for example, substantial parts of Methodism and the Baptist churches, the child in the church is there in preparation for the day when he will hear the Gospel for himself, and will respond in repentance and faith. For the Baptists, this moment will reach its climax at baptism; for other churches some other kind of profession of faith, whether accompanied by baptism or not, will be the moment when church membership is acquired. In the churches of this general outlook, where infant baptism is practised, it becomes an expression of hope and faith, an anticipation of the child's future response and a celebration of the love and grace of God towards both child and parents. Here the young person who later professes his faith may be thought of as ratifying his church membership, or (more usually) of moving from junior or child membership or 'membership of the Junior church' to membership of the adult church. In Baptist churches, the child dedication ceremonies might signify all these things, baptism itself being reserved for those who choose it for themselves as their personal identification with Christ, and as a symbol of their willingness to follow him in the church.

228. The reformed (Calvanistic and Presbyterian) churches have confessed the theology of the child in the covenant of grace, to which reference has already been made. The child is looked upon as being bound up with his believing parents in covenant with God and the church. 'The promise is to you and to your children' (Acts 2:39) and 'And I will establish my covenant between me and you and your descendants after you' (Genesis

17:7). The child is baptised as a sign and seal of the covenant, and becomes a 'presumptive Christian'. He is presumed in faith, on the basis of the covenant calling, to be regenerated. For if the covenant is given to the child, so are the blessings of the covenant, and these include forgiveness of sins, fellowship with God and the gift of the Holy Spirit. The child is thus to grow up in the faith, knowing himself as a Christian. Certainly there may be experiences of the conversion type, but these will not be understood as indicating a move from a position of no faith to one of faith. They will rather be stages of his sanctification, or times when grace renews its work in him, a grace which began in him when he was brought into the covenant, and when this was expressed in his baptism.

229. Childhood as a time of innocence is the view which is traditionally found amongst the Quakers, Unitarians, some Congregationalists (others adopted the covenant view), and the descendants of the continental Anabaptists (Mennonites, Hutterites and so on). This view is also combined with a conversion theology, the idea being that childhood is a latent period, of ignorance and innocence. Questions of sin, faith and church membership do not apply to children until they reach the age of understanding, at which point responsibility, moral awareness and the need for repentance and faith arise.

230. It is interesting to see how these traditional denominational theologies of the child are intersected by aspects of modern child study. The romantic view of childhood, in which it is idealised·as the time of purity, is in sharp contrast to the Catholic view of original sin, and Freudian psycho-analysis, with its emphasis upon the sexuality and the passionate emotional life of childhood, runs counter to the 'purity' view. The idea of the stages of childhood development, which we find in late medieval views concerning the 'age of understanding' and which were developed quite elaborately in the Anabaptist theories of childhood's progress, has an obvious parallel in the stage theories of Piaget and Kohlberg, Goldman and Peatling, and it is interesting to note that these are not confined to cognitive development but deal so with emotional maturity and moral awareness. Another contemporary line of research, into the religious experiences of childhood and youth (Edward Robinson and Michael Paffard) throws light upon childhood as a time of deep sensitivity to the world, to beauty and to the numinous. One of the reasons for the rather uncertain state of mind about childhood which we find in the churches today is perhaps that the traditional theologies which interpreted childhood in terms of sin, grace and salvation, have not been related very carefully if at all to the findings and assumptions of modern child study.

THEOLOGICAL THEMES: BAPTISM AND COMMUNION

231. Let us now select some of the theological themes which emerge from a comparative study of the traditional theologies of childhood. In the Orthodox and Catholic churches, the child must be in the church if he is to be saved,

for 'There is no salvation outside the church'. Baptism is the gateway into the church, and the means of passing from the unregenerate condition into the life of grace. Those who are not baptised are therefore not saved, and in the case of unbaptised infants dying in infancy, we find a wide range of approaches. It is probably true to say that the main stream of Catholic though declares that the unbaptised child is excluded from the vision of God, but the severity of the conclusions which might be drawn from this were mitigated by various subsidiary themes. The unbaptised child might enjoy all natural felicity, being in a state of happy although unsanctified existence, since the result of his original sin was to exclude him rather than to actively merit his punishment.

232. Another line of thought lays stress upon the intention or desire of the parents that the child should have been baptised, the desire being acceptable to God in conditions where actual baptism of the infant was prevented by circumstances. Yet another strand speaks of the God-given desire within the infant himself for baptism (i.e. for salvation and communion with God). This view almost meets the Protestant view that unbaptised children are saved, coming as it were around the other side of the mountain. But although these various minor themes offer comfort and even hope to the parent, the main emphasis has continued to be upon the security of the position of the baptised child, who, his sins washed away and so freed from that which would exclude him from the presence of God, is enabled by grace to grow up in the church, as a Christian child, being confirmed at an early age and receiving communion usually well before adolescence. So we see that in this view of Christian childhood, the dominant motifs are the relation between church, salvation and sacraments.

233. We have been speaking of a similarity between the Catholic and Orthodox views of children in the church. When we turn our attention to theories of stage development however the links are between Catholic and Protestant churches. The Orthodox churches, in giving communion to infants, seem to rule out the connection between the sacraments and various periods of 'readiness' in the growing child. In this respect, the Orthodox are in fact closer to the Baptists, except that the one tradition confers all the relevant sacraments upon infancy and the other denies them all to infancy. In the Orthodox churches, the process of Christian upbringing is more a matter of socialisation, and this also corresponds to the early Anabaptist views of a socialisation of children and youth within special communities and schools. With both the Anabaptists and the Orthodox, childhood is a state of innocence, in the one case because the child is purified by the sacraments and is living on the body of Christ in his church, in the other case because the child is in a state of innocent latency and irresponsibility prior to the emergence of the will to sin and the sense of guilt. But in Catholic and main stream Protestant churches (Baptists apart) the sacraments form a developmental hierarchy, beginning with infant baptism, passing through confession and penance and confirmation (the order varies) to participation in the eucharist and finally to marriage.

THEOLOGICAL THEMES: THE COVENANT

234. Another theme of theologies of childhood is that of the covenant. In the thought of many of the reformers, but especially John Calvin, the covenant formed the basis of the child's relation to the Gospel, the Church and to God himself. The covenant, rather than ideas of the link between church membership and salvation, becomes the ground for infant baptism. In the covenant with Abraham, which is the archteypal covenant of grace, children are circumcised as of right, not to bring them into the covenant so much as to signify their place in it, although of course the act of circumcision was itself part of the covenant. The covenant of grace, whereby men, women and children are admitted into fellowship with God and become his people and he their God, is contrasted with the covenant of works, of which the law is the expression. The covenant of grace is continuous under the old dispensation and the new, so that although taking a different form after the incarnation and atonement of Christ, it continues to be the same gracious act in which eternal life is bestowed. Circumcision corresponds to infant baptism, so the children of believers are seen not as sinners, nor as occupying a sort of in-between position, but as heirs of the Kingdom and joint heirs with their parents and with Christ.

235. Since the children are in the covenant, they are apparently regenerated, and their calling and the work of the Holy Spirit in them is ratified by their baptism. Infants are renewed by the Spirit of God, and this progresses in degrees, until the presumptive repentance, expressed in their baptism for the forgiveness of sins, is no longer latent but manifest in their lives. The doctrine recognises the great significance for the child and the church of birth into a Christian family. The family is looked upon as a corporate entity and so the child is already within the realm of grace and in the church. The family then becomes the focus, or rather the means of grace, for the progressive renewal and advancement of the child's spirit and so the theory of Christian child-rearing becomes not merely a pattern of socialisation nor of preparation for early conversion nor only a catechesis or instruction arranged in various stages but a steady enrichment, a Christian nurture in the fullest sense.

BAPTIST VIEWS

236. The position of the Baptists is so distinctive and so interesting that it calls for special comment. In the first place, the Baptists present us with the contrast between the place of the child in the national or regional church and his place in a church which by rejecting infant baptism had cut itself off not only from the life of the main churches but also from the life of the nation. It seems likely that in modern secularised conditions this difference is no longer a very significant one. Three main strands of Baptist life since the sixteenth century may be distinguished. First there has been the continental Anabaptists, then

the English General Baptists, and finally the English Particular Baptists. In the seventeeth century the General and the Particular strands united, the extreme conservative wing of the Particular Baptists merged with the Strict and Particular Baptists who held a vigorous doctrine of predestination. All the groups rejected infant baptism, and all shared certain emphases with other Separatist groups – attitudes towards the ministry, kinds of church government, and the priesthood of all believers. But the theology of the covenant was rejected, although the implications of this rejection for the place of children in the church differed, at least in the sixteenth and seventeenth centuries, before the uniting of the General and the Particular strands.

237. For the General Baptists, who were under the influence not of Calvin but Arminius, the Gospel was the free gift of God to all while sin was seen as personal responsibility atoned for by Christ and appropriated by the individual believer in faith and repentance. So those infants who die in their infancy die within the salvation wrought by Christ for all mankind, and because original sin was distinguished from original guilt, and children do not share in the latter, they die in a state of innocence. Baptism was not only a profession of faith but also an initiation into the church, which was a gathered fellowship of believers.

238. For the Particular Baptists, however, the motif of baptism was different. The Particulars saw baptism as the symbol of identification with Christ in his death and resurrection, a symbol of the new life of the Christian. Like the Reformed Calvinistic churches, the Particular Baptists accepted covenant theology but denied the continuity between the Old and the New covenants, so that circumcision could not be analogous with infant baptism. Baptism stood not for the covenant but for the death and rising with Christ by faith. Like the Calvinistic churches (and like the Anabaptists of the continent) the Particular Baptists emphasised the invisible church, composed of the elect and known only to God, but membership of the visible church was based upon profession of faith. Childhood tended to be less securely grounded in the church with the Particular Baptists than with the General, although even with the General Baptists the link between childhood and the church was not expressed very strongly.

239. After union, the two views on baptism came together. Baptists today recognise baptism as a profession of faith, an identification with Christ in his death and resurrection and as the initiation ceremony of the church. But infant baptism is rejected for very much the same reasons as in the formative period, although infant dedication is widely practised. Children, it is believed, are not ready for faith, do not understand what is required of them, cannot be held responsible for sin, and can only be in a state of preparation for church membership. One must remember that for the Baptists as for the other Protestant churches, baptism is not a requirement for salvation. Baptism is to be sought personally and voluntarily, it being a symbol of an inner change which the seeker now knows has been wrought in his heart. Being a Christian is a matter of Christian discipleship, in which one is committed to Christ and to the fellowship of believers in the church of Christ.

240. The position of the Reformed Baptists is different again. Although the doctrines of election and covenant are taken seriously (hence the title 'Reformed') the continuity between the covenant of the Old Testament and that of the New is completely denied. Children are consequently regarded as being not Christian until they are converted. Instruction is necessary so that the children of believers do not grow up with a false sense of security, believing themselves to be Christian when they are not. The Reformed Baptists thus believe that the Calvinist view of the child in the covenant does a grave dis-service to childhood. The child is lost, alienated from God, and only the Gospel of salvation can remedy this state. To encourage children in the belief that they were in the church or were Christian children would be but to breed false hopes in them. These then are Calvinists with a non-Calvinist view of childhood. Infant baptism is rejected and both church and parents are placed under a grave responsibility of evangelising their children, so that they may be born again.

241. The rejection of society was more extreme in the case of the continental Anabaptists, who formed special communes in which Christian socialisation took place in sharp contra-distinction to the surrounding world. Infant baptism was rejected and a series of events was laid out which formed the path from the innocence of childhood to the maturity of Christian youth. This sequence consisted in the preaching of the World, its hearing, repentance, faith and finally baptism. The emergence of self-will, the ability to distinguish good from evil, the manifestation of a good (or bad) conscience towards God were amongst the signs which marked progression through these stages. Great importance was attached to understanding and to obedience. Baptism and profession of faith came as the climax to a self-surrender offered in obedience to God. Original sin in infancy was of no significance until manifestated in acts of actual sin, and infants dying were within the universal grace of God, their fate being left with God, although Anabaptists tended to be optimistic. Until the day when their free, voluntary self-surrender to God was symbolised in their baptism, children were to be disciplined, in a strict community life.

242. Thus various Baptist groups, though differing in some things, shared a view of childhood: the child had not reached the age of understanding, could not show faith in a mature way, was not to be baptised and was not a church member. He was in preparation until that day when he would be converted to the faith, become a Christian and join the church. Being a Christian was a matter of personal discipleship. This conversion view of childhood has been shared by some paedo-Baptists, *e.g.* many Methodists and other evangelical groups. At root it is a view of the church and of the doctrines of sin and grace.

243. All these traditional views, some of them still very much alive, have something to contribute towards an understanding of what it is or might be to grow up as a Christian. Certainly none of them is necessarily at variance with critical openness, which works with problems and ideas distinctively modern. But in some way or other, it is important to be able to conceive of

childhood being a time of Christian growth. It is quite possible that the various theological positions, such as that which emphasises the importance of faith and personal response, can still be defended even while allowing that children may still be Christians. Perhaps the application of the criteria can be extended to include childhood without the criteria for Christian life and faith themselves having to be reconsidered. It may be, for example, that when the various objections to the idea of Christian childhood are reconsidered, some can be met without demanding too heavy a theological price from those traditions in which childhood in the church is less secure.

Summary: The traditional denominational theologies see the place of childhood reflected through doctrines of the church, sacraments (especially baptism), grace and salvation, conversion and the inner workings of the Holy Spirit. All have something to offer a modern theory of Christian upbringing, but the need for a doctrine of Christian childhood in the church remains paramount.

POTENTIAL OR ACTUAL CHRISTIANS ?

244. There are various objections to the idea of Christian childhood. The first is that children are only potential Christians. The distinction between potential and actual, between promise and fulfilment, is basic for Christian theology, and we have already seen how this tension became the inspiration for critical testing in the early church. Some early Protestant thought, as we have also seen, declared that in a mysterious way God did indeed regenerate the hearts of baptised infants, so that the promise and the fulfilment were already together in the sacrament. Their emphasis upon the idea of the sovereignty of divine grace, or upon the need for individual response, led many Protestant churches away from the idea that baptism could be the *agent* of actualisation, and in the form of the child dedication ceremony, the intentions of the parents become uppermost, the child being considered entirely within the realm of hope. Of course, all theologies of infant baptism have to some extent been anticipatory, seeing baptism as the seal of a process of justification and sanctification which would be one unbroken process of future growth in grace, or considering baptism as the first rung of the sacramental ladder of perfection, being completed by confirmation, or by the reception of the Holy Spirit or by 'full' membership.

245. Although the achievements of the baby during his first weeks of life are considerable, they are small compared with his potential, or, if we think of personhood as gift and as achievement, the element of gift seems to be greater in the case of the baby than the element of personhood won through struggle. However, this consideration must not lead us into exaggeration. Potential and actual are not to be thought of as two sides of a pair of scales, the balance between which can be simply observed at any given stage of life. It is only in achievement necessarily leaves unrealised many other potentials which will now never be realised, a lot of potential is by definition

unrealisable, and therefore can hardly be placed in the scales against the achievement. You daughter's potential for becoming the bride of Tom and Dick will (you may trust) never be realised now that she has actually become the bride of Fred. So we may ask at what point is the divide between the potential and actual to be seen in our lives. Are we potential Christians until our death? Or until our full sanctification? or our baptism?

246. Perhaps the whole notion of a dividing line between potential and actual is mistaken. If Christian life is to be thought of as a process of growth, the ratio of potential growth to actual growth will always be changing and we will never know whether or at what point: what we have been given outweights what we still have to receive. So to speak as if a significant line could be drawn between childhood and adulthood in these terms is surely mistaken. We know that many children have great potential as Christians because we see Christian faith actualised in their lives, or we have grounds for faith that some actualisation has taken place. But in a sense, because their choices and experiences have opened up new possibilities for them, adults have even greater potential. Potential is not a fixed sum which is given to us at birth.

CONVERSION AND CHILDREN

247. A second type of objection comes from some of those who think that without an experience of conversion it is impossible to speak with confidence of being a Christian. This view would not deny that children may become Christians, but it will be on the basis of conversion. Before that takes place, the child is to be evangelised. Now it is certain that vivid and meaningful religious experiences take place in childhood, even in early childhood. The difficulty arises only when it is insisted that without these, and indeed without a particular kind of religious experience, taking the form of a crisis, Christian living cannot begin. It seems more realistic in view of the variety of Christian religious experience, and more open to the range of the divine grace, if we merely say that at some point or at various points of the development of Christian life, whether in childhood, youth or in adulthood, there will usually be crises, periods of sudden growth or illumination. The teacher and parent will not be surprised if these occur, and may be concerned if by late adolescence no formation of conviction has taken place, but he will not claim that such crises are the *only* evidence of God's calling. The theology which emphasises conversion is a protest against the formality and conventionality of much religious life, and it has an important role to play. But it must not be allowed to overshadow other equally important aspects of Christian faith.

248. It is worth pointing out that the theology of the child in the covenant or grace does not suggest that one can be *born* a Christian by natural descent. The idea is not that Christian faith can be passed on or inherited biologically. Rather, the child in the covenant is a child of promise. We have reason to believe that our children are called by God into fellowship with himself

because he has promised to give himself to them. This promise is first declared in the Old Testament, fulfilled in the teaching and ministry of Jesus and confirmed by the practice of the church. The relation between the generations is itself thought of a a part of the gracious bounty of God. He is to be our God and our children's God. Just as, in Reformed thought, baptism is not thought of instrumentally, as if it were the *cause* or the means of the reception into the church, so parenthood is not thought of instrumentally either. Parenthood is not the *cause* of a child being a Christian child. If this were the case, there would indeed by a claim that flesh and blood could inherit the Kingdom, or that one could become a child of God by the will of the flesh. But the teaching of the reformers was that such children are children of Abraham, of grace through the promise. The faith of Christian parents is not in themselves as the progenitors of Christian children, but in the promise of God that their children will, by his own free mercy and calling, be held within his love. If this were more clearly understood, it would do at least something to remove what has often been a serious offence to those who, had the reformed teaching really been as they imagined, would have been fully justified in rejecting it and insisting upon conversion.

INTELLECTUAL DEMANDS OF CHURCH MEMBERSHIP

249. The most important and widely encountered objection to Christian childhood is the cognitive or intellectualist difficulty. To be a Christian, the argument goes, one must have certain beliefs, such as belief in God and Christ. To have the beliefs one must first possess the concepts. But the concepts depend, for their acquisition, upon earlier concepts (*e.g.* 'Heavenly Father' depends upon 'father' and 'heaven') so one cannot consider a person a Christian until he has undergone a fairly lengthy period of mental growth. The argument might also run: to be a Christian is to worship God through Christ. But this must be done deliberately and consciously, otherwise it is not *done* at all, in the sense that such worship would not be an intended action. The same is true of following Christ, or whatever criterion one took of Christian discipleship. But little children and babies cannot meet any of these demands. Such young children are therefore neither Christian nor non-Christian but reside in a sort of preparatory period, pending their emotional and mental development.

250. But this rod strikes too many backs. Are we to say that the senile cannot be Christians? Must we all be fearful of losing our status as Christians in our extreme old age, or whenever our minds have deteriorated to a certain point? What about the retarded? Is the church's ministry to them to be seen in the same light as the church's work in taking care of animals? What about persons who are intuitive or concrete thinkers? Is being a Christian open only to abstract thinkers? Will not this approach lead us into a kind of gnosticism, in which only the intellectually able will become the illuminated?

251. The intellectualist objection also runs into trouble on the grounds that it exchanges the divine grace for a human achievement in the determination of who is to count as a Christian. It offers as criteria a series of attainments. But what are the criteria for the selection of these criteria? If we take Christianity seriously as it announces itself to us, then, whether we use the idea of God as giving himself in the covenant or in the sacraments or in religious experience, we have conditions which children can meet. If we are to speak of some kind of response to God as being necessary in being a Christian, then we may ask whether the infant in the womb has some kind of response to his mother. Certainly the newly born child has a very vivid response to his mother. Now, whatever response to God may mean, there seem insufficient grounds for denying that an infant may be responding to God through his response to his mother. It is only if 'response' is confined to intellectual belief and language that this claim creates a difficulty for the status of little children. But sayings such as 'Out of the mouths of babes and sucklings thou has brought perfect praise' (Matthew 21:16) and 'Thou hast hidden these things from the wise and understanding and revealed them to babes' (Matthew 11:25) suggest that this is a needless constriction to place upon the meaning of response to God.

Summary: The various objections to the idea of children being Christians (the 'potential' argument, the 'conversion' argument and the 'intellectual' argument) although making useful points must not be allowed to obscure the reasons for believing children may be Christians. Each of the objections also carries unacceptable consequences for other aspects of Christian life and faith if it is taken to the point of denying that children may be Christians.

252. So far we have seen that children *may* be Christians, and that we have every reason to think that certain children, namely the children in the church, who stand under the address of the Gospel and are included by promise and sacrament within the body of Christ, are *actually* Christians. They are not to be thought of as the church of the future, nor as being only attached in some vague way, as if they were merely adherents, nor placed in a special category like a cradle roll. They are heirs together with us adults in the grace of the Christian life. They are not to be made central in the church, any more than are old people, or men, or women. They are simply to be considered a part of the church, as much a part as any other class or group with special characteristics and special needs. And because the child is within the church, he is to be nurtured like a member of any other age group, bearing in mind any special needs. One of the special circumstances of children is that they are dependent upon the adults with whom they live, and these are normally their parents. We now turn to a consideration of the role of Christian parents in the nurturing of Christian children.

Chapter 13

CHRISTIAN PARENTHOOD AND GENERAL NURTURE

253. What do we mean by 'family'? The typical family, as pictured so often in television advertisements or in story books, consists of father, mother and two or three children. Many children are indeed brought up in just such families, but many are not. Let us consider some of the following figures, in order to picture in our minds the situation about which we are enquiring. In England and Wales there are approximately nine million children attending schools. There estimated to be approximately 1.5 million children living in one parent families in the United Kingdom. Some 120,000 children in the United Kingdom are officially in care. The number of children between five and ten left unsupervised during the school holidays has been conservatively estimated to be 300,000 and the number left unsupervised after school until parents come home from work has been put at 225,000.

254. This is not only the background against which the Christian nurture of children is taking place, it is often also the foreground. In the churches, as in society at large, many children are being brought up by one parent only, sometimes an unmarried mother, sometimes a parent who has been bereaved. There are those whose parents are separated or divorced. The child whose parents live apart will live for most of the time with only one parent but may regularly stay with the other. Such a child is not so much a 'one parent child' as a 'two family child'. There are growing numbers of such families in the church. The church has a special duty towards them. Christian girls who are unmarried mothers and Christians who have experienced marital breakdown often feel so guilty or so unsure of the attitude of other Christians towards them that they exclude themselves from church life. The first thing they need is to find a matter of fact acceptance, and so an encouragement to stay within the fellowship of the church, and to receive like everyone else all the healing and support which a Christian community can provide. Second, they need to see that their a-typical families are not for that reason any less truly Christian than any other, and that whatever their special difficulties, relationships within their families need be no less loving and fruitful.

255. We are faced then with a wide range of different family shapes even before we start to think of the more special arrangements of children's homes and other institutions for children living with adults. A family which in all other respects normal, in that it consists of children and their two natural parents living together, may have amongst its members fostered children, adopted children, and others attached ot it temporarily or only semi-permanently. We must also remember the special problems presented for the Christian nurture in their families of children who are physically, mentally or

emotionally handicapped. There may be some directions in which some of such children will never reach maturity, in that they may continue to need throughout their lives forms and degrees of care and attention which the normal child will sooner or later do without. The way we nurture such children will depend to some extent upon the possible future we can open them up for them, and those which we cannot. The relationship between a Christian parent and a handicapped child can not only be as loving and as deeply Christian as any other but may frequently become much more so. Nevertheless it will certainly present different features from the relationship between a parent and a normal child. The relationship between a parent and a child who is only temporarily a member of his or her family can also be just as loving and as Christian as any other; but again it will be different from many other parent/child relationships. All these varieties, and more, are likely to be met with in our churches, and if we are to speak usefully of Christian nurture within the family we must not speak of it in ways which are appropriate only to the 'normal' or 'typical' family. The 'family' for our present purposes, means *any association or relationship in which a child is cared for and brought up by an adult*. A family may also be two or three elderly people living together or a home without children, but we will not, in this report, consider the Christian nurture which such families exercise.

Summary: Within the churches a wide variety of family types exist and this variety should be more readily accepted. We make no assumptions about 'normal' families but regard as a family any association or relationship in which a child is cared for and brought up by an adult.

THE CHRISTIAN FAMILY

256. What do we mean by a *Christian* family? Once more, when we look round our churches, and at the real families from which our members come, the 'norm' of two committed Christian parents, living together and bringing up their children, turns out to be no norm at all. The parents in families attached to the church are often highly unequal in their degree of commitment. It is very common to find only one of them deeply committed to the church, while the attitude of the other may be anything from warm but uncommitted support to outright hostility. Sometimes this situation has arisen because a person with Christian convictions has married someone without, but very frequently it happens because one partner is drawn into church life after marriage. In other ways too a family may be divided. It may contain older children who, having been brought up within the church, have not maintained their connection.

257. A good case can be made out for saying that the church should regard as a Christian family *any family which has at least one Christian member*. Since we are concerned with Christian nurture we shall naturally be thinking mainly of the family which has at least one Christian parent. A Christian family, for our purposes, is a domestic arrangement in which *at least one child is*

being Christianly nurtured by at least one Christian adult. At the same time, it is worth noting that there are families where first the children have become attached to the church and have reached Christian conviction, and one or both parents have followed. In such a family, we may ask, who has been nurtured by whom?

258. In speaking like this of 'Christian families' we do not of course assume that the name Christian can be foisted upon those members of the family who may choose otherwise, but that the family in which at least one member is a Christian is a family which is relevant to the concerns of Christian nurture. This relevance is not of a statistical nature, or even merely pastoral. The spiritual unity of those who live intimately with one another in peace must also be recognised. The natural order of mutual love and care is a mirror of the divine life, and this should be taken seriously by any who have been over-impressed by Paul's advice that Christians should not 'be mismated with unbelievers' (2 Corinthians 6:14). For in 1 Corinthians 7:12-16 Paul specifically speaks of the problem of the divided family, and his advice is that the Christian should not feel obliged to separate. The circumstances must be considered, and verse 15 shows that if the family was to separate on religious grounds, the initiative for this should come from the non-Christian members (see para. 292). A Christian family is one in which all the members have a certain intimacy with Christ through their intimacy with one who is part of the body of Christ. There is therefore a real solidarity of the Christian family even when not all members of it acknowledge or desire the name Christian as individuals.

ECUMENICAL FAMILIES

259. Most of the divided families in which at least one member is a Christian will have other members who are merely indifferent. There will be cases where a Christian is married to someone whose commitment is to atheism or humanism, but in the majority of families, the non-Christian members are likely to be apathetic rather than hostile. But the situation in which partners in a marriage belong to different branches of the church will be frequently found. Life in such 'mixed marriages', as they used to be called, is much less trying than it once was, but it is probably still true that differences of religious *belief* are more devisive than differences of preferences and habits in *worship*. If mother goes to mass at 7.00 a.m. while father breaks bread with the Brethren at 11.00 the problems raised for the Christian nurture of the children are likely to be less severe than if mother insists upon the literal inerrancy of scripture while father insists on the authority of the Pope.

260. The crucial question here is whether the members of the family are willing to accept each other as Christians and to use their differences positively for the Christian nurture of the children. Honesty with the children is surely the first step. The differences must be spoken of, and it must be plainly seen that Christians disagree about such things. It must be further

seen that the differences are not unimportant, but they remain alternatives *within* the Christian faith. They very presence of such alternatives, if handled seriously, honestly and yet with humorous acceptance, will be an enrichment of the children's Christian environment. This is especially true if we consider that Christian nurture should take place, if possible, in an ecumenical rather than a denominational context. Just because it cuts across the denominational lines, which are often more sharply drawn in the churches, the ecumenical families (let us call them that, rather than 'mixed') have an advantage over the denominational confined congregations.

RELIGIOUS DIVISION IN FAMILIES

261. The problems may become more severe if one partner refuses to accept that the way of the other is a truly Christian way. Christian critical openness has been lost in such a situation. It is lost to the Christian nurture process in that family because of the one partner who rejects critical openness in his or her own relations with the faith represented by the partner. But might not any one of us find himself in the position of the one who becomes the intolerant partner? What of the orthodox Christian who is married to a member of a small, fanatical sect, or whose partner becomes converted to such a sect, and sees his or her children drawn away into a narrow, contentious and constricting movement? What of the Christian whose partner becomes a convert to a political creed which on Christian grounds must be regarded as repellant and immoral?

262. It is certainly possible to think of such situations, and to experience them, in which the divisions became intolerable and the possibility of a Christian nurture seriously impaired, but they do not set limits to Christian critical openness can be strong and penetrating, and are not merely, if at all, benevolent in an all-accommodating way. Christian critical openness is a stance of enquiry, which is onward moving. It reaches conclusions which it holds with vigour and determination (which we earlier called dogmatism) and then advances to further enquiry, sometimes re-examining the earlier conclusions. This attitude is not only compatible with the firm rejection of malicious and repugnant alternatives but seems to demand it. So there may well be extreme cases in which the spirit of loving criticism and free enquiry will reach a point where values greater than the unity of the family are at stake. The 'two family child' may have more of an opportunity to learn of the Christian way in one of his families than he had when he only had one family (see para. 300).

263. There will also be those families in which a Christian man or woman has married a Jew, a Muslim, or a member of some other great world faith. Such marriages may become rather more common in Britain. Just as the idea of an ecumenical Christian nurture may turn the ecumenical Christian marriage into a Christian nurture advantage, so, if critical openness is

regarded as an ideal in Christian nurture, the presence in the family of another great world faith can also, in favourable conditions, become an advantage. In reckoning such families to be Christian families, one must also agree, by the same logic, that they are Islamic or Jewish families as well. In situations where one is *met by* intolerance, the situations will be similar to those described in the previous paragraphs, whilst in situations where one is *extending* the intolerance, one must always ask if the intolerance is the result of mere ignorance or prejudice, or whether it has been achieved by and through the practice of Christian love and criticism (see para. 170). The distinction will seldom be made easily.

264. Even in the family in which the division is between some Christian members and other who are simply not involved in Christian life and faith, there are bound to be some tensions of a kind which will not be found so acutely in the family which is unanimously Christian. There must often be tension for the Christian members between their commitment to their Christian way and their commitment to the rest of the family. They cannot commit the whole family to a way of life which accords with the convictions of only some of its members. The Christian in the divided family must strike a very careful balance. He must maintain his Christian way of life firmly enough to be a real witness to the other members of his family, but not so rigidly that he alienates them. In short, he must display his love for Christ, but not (if this is at all possible) in a way that calls in question his love for other members of his family or his respect for their different ways. Where and how this balance is struck is very much a matter for the individual concerned. The church ought not to make things more difficult for him by merely urging him to deeper commitment. The Christian in the divided family needs the church's sympathy and support, not merely exhortation and greater demands.

265. Within the very broad limits of the few extreme situations, Christian nurture in the divided family will perforce be open. The child in such a family will be very well aware that various ways of life are possible, possible for him. Then a Christian mother will not wish to present Christianity to her child in such a way as to decrease respect for a non-Christian father. A Christian father will not want to shake the security and confidence of his children in their non-Christian mother. The nurture takes place within and by means of the mutual love and respect of the people in a divided family. One must also remember that all that is happening to the child in the divided family is that he is meeting in his own home alternatives which most children will meet eventually. This enables us to see that in the family which is unanimously Christian, the need for critical openness is no less great. It is just a little less obvious.

Summary: Just as we cannot assume a standard family structure so we cannot assume a standard Christian family. Any family in which one member is a Christian is a Christian family and the situation of religiously divided families must be considered with sensitivity. But openness is necessary for all Christian families, whether unanimous or not.

GENERAL NURTURE

266. General Nurture includes everything which we do for our children which enables them to grow and develop. Christian nurture includes everything which we do for our children which enables them to grow and develop as Christians. What then are the extra things which a Christian parent does for his children are *exactly the same* as those which a non-Christian parent does. The Christian bank manager does not have a special Christian way of setting out his accounts, or use any special Christian arithmetic for adding up his figures. Neither does the Christian farmer use special Christian fertilizers. Both of them do exactly what other bank managers or other farmers do, but they do it with the integrity and the consideration and the cheerfulness that spring from faith. Likewise, the Christian parent has no uniquely Christian way of cooking the dinner or bathing the baby. In spite of this, it may still be true that before we ever get to the extra ten per cent of things that only Christian parents do for their children, our children have already been won or lost by the way we managed the other ninety. Let us therefore focus first on that large area of general nurture relates to the special nurture in which only Christians engage.

267. Any parent, if he is a normal human being, loves his own children – loves them whether they are a help or a nuisance; loves them whether they are good or naughty. There are, to be sure, tragic cases where the bond between parent and child appears not to have been properly formed and where the parent does not respond to the child in the ways that seem to the rest of us so natural and instinctive. Further, the parent who does make the natural attachment to his or her child may not always express that attachment *wisely*. There are many ways of damaging children which fall far short of baby-battering, and some of them are the ways not of hatred but of mistaken love. Love can rot a child's teeth by giving it all the sweets it desires, or stunt its emotional development by refusing to give it the independence its growing soul needs.

268. Perhaps more relevant to the majority of us is the observation that many perfectly normal parents have times when they *imagine* they don't love their children. A mother, or other housebound parent, may find herself bored by her children's unrelenting presence and conversation; resentful of the demands they make, and occasionally may be so frustrated that she or he could actually say she or he hated them. But if, even when she was feeling her worst, one of her children was in real distress or danger, the mother's normal feelings would reassert themselves with remarkable speed. In spite of all her frustrations the *fundamental* attitude of such a mother towards her children is one of love. We can safely say, then, in spite of the fact that love does not always express itself wisely, that parents normally and naturally love their children. Our general nurturing of our children is a spontaneous expression of that love.

269. But our nurturing of our children does not only express our love *for* them, it elicits a response of love *from* them. And this is a very important part

of the nurturing process. The most obvious elements in the general nurturing process are the ones which concern *physical* nurture. Parents give their children food, keep them clean, and so on. But normal parents also spend a good deal of time in other activities with their children; talking to them even when they are far too young to understand a word; smiling at them; making silly baby noises at them. As they get older, of course, they indulge in other forms of play and of social interaction. These activities are not some sort of optional extra to parenthood. They are an important part of the general nurturing process. Experiments have shown that young animals, if they have every physical need supplied but are denied social and emotional relationships, grow into adults that are unable to make normal responses to their own kind. The instances of human individuals who have been deprived of love in their early years demonstrate the same, that those who have not been shown affection cannot display it. Love is something that has to be learnt. The tiny baby, lying in his pram or cot, is already a social being. He quickly learns to respond by smiling when he is smiled at, and to make noises in reply when people speak to him. Equally important, he discovers that when *he* initiates the smiling and the gurgling and the chuckling, other people respond to him. He learns that he can make things happen just by appealing to people, and he learns to respond to appeals by others. Throughout his formative years these lessons are reinforced a thousand times a day. So from those around him (and that usually means parents and it may include other children) every child learns what love is, how to respond to love and how to express love.

GOD IS LOVE

270. Now 'God is love' (1 John 4:8). So, simply by doing what comes naturally to parents, we are mediating God to our children. All this is true whether we are Christians or non-Christians. This may seem a surprising conclusion, but there are in fact good religious reasons, good biblical reaons, why we should *expect* Christian and non-Christian parents to be behaving, at this point, in much the same way.

271. The Bible is full of commandments. Some are difficult to fulfil, and some are very difficult indeed. But some of the most important are very easy. According to the book of Genesis (1:28) the first commandment God gave men after he created them was: 'Be fruitful and multiply, and fill the earth'. That is to say, the command to fall in love, and to produce and bring up a family, is the first commandment of all. But we hardly every think of it as a commandment, because God has so constructed us that most of us have the very greatest enthusiasm for obeying it. When we do what comes naturally to parents we are in fact responding to a divine command, and even those 'who have not the law do by nature what the law requires' (Romans 2:14). In nurturing our children in the way that comes naturally to parents we show them love, and show them how to love. Whoever shows his children love, shows them God. All parents can do it. Christian parents see themselves as

doing it. This one reason, incidentally, why there is still a solid basis for partnership between a Christian and a non-Christian parent in the upbringing of their children.

272. The Bible suggests other ways of making the point. It tells us that we are made in the image of God (Genesis 1:26). Whatever our shortcomings, there are some things about us that are still distinctly God-shaped, and nowhere is this likeness more apparent than when we act in our capacity as parents. No one takes this parallel between the human parent and the heavenly Father with more seriousness than Jesus. He assumes that we can get important clues about what God is like simply by observing ourselves and our fellow human beings. In Matthew 7:7-11 he says:

'If you then, who are evil, know how to give good gifts to your children, how much more will your Father who is in heaven give good things to those who ask him!'

Here Jesus is arguing: 'Watch any ordinary parent in action and you will know something about how God acts'. Let us note, in passing, that Jesus is not saying that God is *exactly like* a human parent, but that we can grasp something about God from observing the *imperfect example* of the human parent. This is a point to which we shall have to return.

273. So then, by being ordinary parents, we are offering our children these clues about God. We are also offering them the basic human experiences without which the religious language they may encounter later will make no sense at all. When eventually someone does tell our children about God, and about God's love and care for them, such talk will only have meaning for them insofar as they have learnt what love and care are from ourselves. Religious language, when the child meets it, will only have content for him if it has been given content by his experience of human relationships. If we have carried out the *general* nurture of the child as good parents are meant to do, then when we do at last come to the special nurture, the extra ten per cent which is *specifically* Christian, it will largely be a matter of putting religious labels on things which the child already knows.

Summary: Christian and non-Christian parents alike share in a general nurture towards their children. The loving care of this normal parental nurturing is part of God's self-giving towards children and forms the basis of their response to him.

UNCONDITIONAL LOVE

274. There are two further aspects of general nurture which are of special importance as the raw material of religious experience: the *unconditional* nature of love within the family, and *nurture for independence* (see para. 280). In considering the conditional nature of love within the family, we note that the child who is brought up by normal, loving parents learns that, whatever may be the standards by which he is judged in the great world outside, his family do not love him because he has a nice nature. They will take pleasure

in any beauty or talent or attractiveness of disposition which he may possess, certainly, but they do not love him *because* of these things. They love him for no better reason than that he is theirs. The child knows, in a word, that his family's love for him is a love which he does not have to deserve, and which he can therefore count on. The experience of such a love, which shines on the just and the unjust, the responsible and the irresponsible or prodigal, which does not have to be merited, is essential if we are ever to grasp, or be grasped by, the love of God in Christ. It is not itself, of course, *religious* experience, but it is the vital material out of which Christian understanding is formed.

275. This unconditional love within the family shows itself spontaneously in *forgiveness.* To call it 'forgiveness' is to make it sound more formal and deliberate than it ever normally is. In ordinary family life people rarely have occasion to say, in so many words, 'I forgive you'. It rarely *needs* to be said, if it is genuinely felt. In family life we irritate each other quite often. Individuals feel 'put out' sometimes. Tempers get lost; hard words are sometimes said; misunderstandings arise. Each of us sometimes gets preoccupied with his own problems and is less sympathetic than he might be to the problems of the others in the household. But in the normal family – certainly, one would like to think, in the normal Christian family – grievances do not get carried forward. People do not hold things against each other. The fact that our children behaved like little horrors yesterday does not affect our attitude to them today, and they do not appear to think any less of us in the morning because we were less than fair to them at bedtime last night. Brought up in such a family the child learns that he can in all ordinary circumstances take forgiveness for granted. He sees that his parents' love for him, like their love for each other, is resilient enough to absorb the shocks that it is exposed to daily, and he learns to display the same sort of love himself.

276. If I dent my car it stays dented, until quite deliberate (and expensive) measures are taken to restore it. If I bruise myself, then without my doing anything consciously about it at all the buise heals, and within a short time it will be impossible to tell that it was ever there. In the wear and tear of ordinary family life we hurt each other quite often. They are mostly little hurts, but sometimes not so little. But if family relationships are healthy the hurts are like bruises, not dents. 'Forgiveness', in this context, does not means anything so self-conscious as saying about this or that individual office, 'I forgive you', but rather that permanent state of willingness to make fresh starts which characterises healthy family relationships. When we encounter the complex and apparently technical language of the New Testament, when it speaks about reconciliation, justification and expiation, it is the experience of forgiveness within the family and between friends which gives body to what is being said. Whether we understand Pauline theologising or not, we can all understand the argument that those who love us are constantly ready to write off the past and start again, and that if God loves us he can hardly do less. So once more, what we are offering our children by behaving in the way that all decent parents do, are experiences which are not themselves religious, but

which can readily be put into religious words and which provide the content for religious statements.

277. In describing such aspects of general nurture as being normal and natural, and as things which parents tend to do just as parents, we do not mean to suggest that many children will not have quite different experiences of parenthood. There are those who feel that they have been rejected by their parents because they did not pass a certain examination, were not as good at something as a brother or talented sister, did not share their parent's dearest interests and so on. And in remarking that it is essential for a later appreciation of the divine love that children should grow up in a love which is unconditional we do not mean that there will never be any way in which the defects of family life may not be compensated for by some other experience which a child or young person may have in growing up. The unconditional love may be found through friends or through some other adults, if the parents should fail. There are many serene and mature Christian adults to whom the grace of God came in spite of terribly unhappy experiences in childhood. But it remains the case that the spontaneous affection from parent to child, when not thwarted or distorted by ambition, jealousy and bitterness, is for most children the simplest and most secure way of being grounded in the beliefs and expectations which Christian nurture should later fulfil.

278. Nothing said in these pages is intended to suggest that Christian faith, even if it is shared by all members of a family, is an infallible recipe for a harmonious, rich and beautiful family life. Christian families suffer from tensions just as other families do. Their members may have just as many difficulties in making adjustments to each other as members of other families. All families, Christian or non-Christian, unless they are very exceptional indeed, go through rough patches when relationships are strained. In some families the strains become so great that the relationships reach breaking point. There is no special providence which protects Christian families and ensures that for them this point is never reached; though it might be expected that Christian families would make more strenuous efforts than most to avoid reaching it.

279. Indeed, when strains and tensions *are* felt, the Christian family may actually in some respects feel them more acutely than many non-Christian families would. For the parents are likely to accuse themselves: 'We are supposed to be *Christian* parents. We should not be losing our tempers with our children'. And ever member will feel: 'We are a Christian family. We ought not to be having rows with each other'. They thus added to whatever burdens they may be bearing an additional burden of guilt. But this is simply one aspect of an inescapable Christian predicament. The Christian constantly creates difficulties simply by expecting more of himself. The extra burden of Christian guilt is a meausre of the extra standard he has imposed on himself. Moreover, the fact that he feels the guilt is itself the first sign of grace. When the members of a Christian family feel that they ought not, as Christians, to be behaving like this, they are judging themselves, that they be

not judged of the Lord. And the cure for this extra burden is the forgiveness of which our faith assures us. The Christian family may not have fewer rows than its non-Christian neighbours, but it will make better new beginnings, because its members will know that they are not only forgiving each other, but sharing the forgiveness of Christ.

Summary: It is in normal, general nurture that the child learns of a love which does not have to be earned and of a forgiveness which is always extended. This is an important basis for his religious growth.

NURTURE FOR INDEPENDENCE

280. The second feature of general nurture which is of particular significance for religion is that it is *nurture for independence*. The relationship between the nurtured and the nurturer is not a static one. It changes and develops as the child grows towards independence and maturity, and indeed its aim is to foster that very growth. Whatever the relationship between parent and child at any given time, the child is busy growing out of it and into a fresh one. This constant change makes demands on the parent to do some growing on his own account. To nurture a child is a maturing experience for the nurturer too. Let us look at some examples of how this happens.

281. The young child is virtually never away from its parents or some other caring adult except when asleep. Whatever he does, his parents (one or both) are likely to be aware of. Then he goes to school, or perhaps playgroup, and immediately he has a private area of life; private, that is, from his parents. It quickly dawns on him that there is now an area of his life into which his parents have no automatic right of entry, and which they can know relatively little about unless he tells them. He may rejoice in his new found privacy by telling stories about what goes on at school; stories which vary from the plausible to the totally incredible, but which either way may bear little relation to the facts. This is the beginning of his independence.

282. Later, the child may acquire skills which the parents have never acquired, or in other ways move into areas of experience where they cannot readily follow. The child so naturally assumes that anything which he knows the parents must know too that it may be some time before he really grasps the fact that this is not always so. The child of musically uneducated parents who begins to learn a musical instrument may for a long time continue to ask them questions ('Should that be a b flat?' or 'How does the timing of this tune go?') before it sinks into his head that they really do not know the answers, and that in this particular field he really does know more than they do. Or the non-swimming parent may read his child's essay describing her feelings as she dives from the high diving board and realise that already she has gone where he will never follow. That there should be such areas where the child moves out of the parents' range and depth is very important for both of them,

105

because a healthy nurturing relationship should never be an entirely one-sided one. In these areas where the child may quite early move beyond the parent the normal relationship is reversed. We have to ask *him* about things which he knows and understands and we do not. This one of the ways in which nurturing becomes an experience of mutual growth. It also prepares us for the bigger adjustments in the parent/child relationship which have to come later on. It helps parent and child to see and accept each other as people in their own right. It thus helps them to respect each other's autonomy. The child does not for ever go on reflecting the values and opinions of his parents. A proper nurture welcomes his growing independence of mind, and encourages it. Proper parental love is a liberating love, a love that sets our children free to be themselves, not copies or reflections of us.

283. Now all this is important from a Christian point of view because once again the relationship between parent and child is a model relationship between God and his creation. We find this in the Gospels in the story of the prodigal son (Luke 15:11-24). In that parable there is nothing really remarkable about the way in which the father welcomes the son home. This is Jesus' point. Isn't this the way we *expect* fathers to behave? Why then should we imagine our Father in heaven to react any differently? What is less typical of fathers is the way in which the father in the parable lets the son go in the first place. Here is a son who is virtually wishing his father dead, so that he can have his share of the estate while he is still young enough to enjoy it. The father in the story goes further than most in allowing his children to make their own mistakes. His love is both a love that forgives the mistakes, and a love which gives the freedom that allows the mistakes to happen.

284. In the Old Testament a similar statement is being made in the story of the fall (Genesis 3). The love that God shows his creation is the same love that gives freedom. He allows mankind to make their own decisions. And yet they are accountable for those decisions. When they go wrong God does not simply scrub everything out and re-start the game. He allows men to live with the results of their mistakes, though in his mercy he gives them help in doing so, and indicates how they might eventually make their failures the basis for achievements. The wise parent, in nurturing for independence, allows his children that freedom with accountability that God allows us all.

285. Once more, there is nothing specifically Christian about nurturing a child for independence. A non-Christian parent may do it as well as a Christian one, but the child who has been so nurtured will have direct experience of a relationship which later he may learn the religious words to describe. But not all parents are wise, and many children will have the experience of being over-protected, or given insufficient room to develop because anxious or insecure parents were trying to relive their own lives in them, trying to do all the things they had wanted to do themselves but had failed. It may be a particular danger for Christian parents in their Christian nurture of their children that they feel hurt or rejected when their growing children come to have views of religious faith which are not the same as theirs.

An understanding of the role of Christian critical openness in Christian nurture may help such parents to have freedom and to extend freedom to their children. But again, as with unconditioned love, it is the nature of the parent-child relation that the young grow to independence, and often the old become dependent again in their own old age. This general condition is the natural ground for the experience of autonomy which should one day be interpreted and fulfilled by Christian nurture.

Summary: General nurture is also nurture for independence. Like nurture for love and forgiveness, this reflects God's treatment of mankind and lays a basis for response to specifically Christian interpretations and experiences.

GENERAL NURTURE AND RELIGIOUS UNDERSTANDING

286. We have spoken of general nurture as providing, not religious experience, but the raw material of religious understanding. When we do offer the child religious words, they will make little sense to him unless he has direct knowledge of the basic human experiences to which they relate. It is rather like teaching a child to read. If we offer him an alphabet book with pictures of steam trains and ink bottles and tell him that E is for engine and I is for ink, we shall be making things very hard for him if he has never seen a steam train or an ink bottle in his life. Ninety per cent, then, of being a good Christian parent is the offering to the child of the ordinary experiences of family life which he will learn the religious words for and the religious dimensions of in due time. Ninety per cent of being a good Christian parent, that is to say, is just being a good parent.

287. There is perhaps a special relevance in all this for the Christian parent in what we have called 'divided families'. What makes good upbringing in such a divided family possible is that the Christian and non-Christian parent can share whole-heartedly in such a large part of the task. One parent may have a Christian understanding of what he or she is doing, and may wish to describe it in Christian words, the other may not, and yet for a very great deal of the time they may be doing exactly the same things and may be subscribing to the same values. This does not remove all difficulties, by any means, and there are still questions to be resolved about those areas of life in which one parent wishes to engage in specifically Christian activities and the other does not. But it does mean that there can be a high degree of co-operation and common purpose, and that the Christian and non-Christian parent can support each other without hypocrisy on either side.

Summary: This normal nurturing provides a basis for religious experience. It is also the unifying sector in the nurture provided by parents one of whom is Christian and the other not.

Children in Church - James Dalrymple 6 yrs

Chapter 14

CHRISTIAN PARENTHOOD AND SPECIAL NURTURE

288. It has several times been hinted in the last few pages that though the Christian parent finds himself for most of the time doing much the same things as the non-Christian parent does, he has a different way of looking at what he is doing. Even when Christian parents are doing just what other parents do they may understand what they are doing in a different way. They may see a different significance in the same actions. They may talk about them in terms which the non-Christian would not use.

289. The fact we sometimes use different words to describe the same things is not a trivial or a superficial matter. The same girl might be described as: 'little and skinny and with whitish hair', or as 'slim, petite and blonde'. Both descriptions might be equally accurate, but the difference is not unimportant. (It is certainly not unimportant to the girl herself.) The label we put on the package may not change the contents, but it may change the way in which the contents are regarded. The knick-knack in the window of the souvenir shop may look rather horrid to our eyes, but if the same knick-knack turns up in a package with a label saying, 'To daddy, with love', we look at in a different way. The words will not have altered our aesthetic judgment, but they have altered the function and significance of the object. We may hand a man a drink and say: 'Cheers!' We may hand the same man a very similar drink and say: 'The blood of Christ, shed for you'. The recipient is identical, the drink very nearly so, and the gesture too. Only the context in which the act takes place, and the words spoken, make it different. Thus, an act which at one time or in one context is an ordinary, secular act, becomes at another time or in another context a profoundly meaningful religious act. An ordinary act becomes a religious act because the people doing it choose so to regard it. Likewise a Christian parent, even when he is doing the ordinary things which all parents do, may see in them a religious dimension which non-Christian parents do not see.

290. The above example prompts a further thought. When Christians come together to share the body and blood of the Lord, one of the things which makes the act so meaningful is that eating and drinking together is not a uniquely *religious* activity. Part of the significance of the sacramental act is that it is an ordinary act transformed. Thus, the Christian parents' general nurture of their children does not lose any of its Christian significance simply because other parents happen to do it too.

291. All parents, when they show their children love, mediate God to those children. Parenthood is a priestly office. Christian parents *see themselves* as mediating God to their children. All parenthood mirrors the Fatherhood of God. Christian parents *see themselves* as mirroring the divine Fatherhood.

All normal parents see the job of bringing up their children as one of great responsibility. Christian parents see themselves as responsible to *God* for the upbringing of their children.

Summary: Although Christian parents share general nurture with all good parents, they interpret it differently. For them, normal parenthood becomes a priestly calling.

SPECIAL NURTURE

292. By 'special' nurture we indicate those things which Christian parents do for their children which other parents do not do. If our own faith is genuine then in some respects we shall express it quite naturally and without having to give the matter any particular thought. However, there are other matters about which we shall need to take quite deliberate decisions. If we are Christians then our children are members of a Christian family (see paras. 256-58), and some consequences follow inevitably from this. We have already said that a Christian family may not be a *unanimously* Christian family. Where this is so, some of the comments made in the following paragraphs will not apply, or will raise particular difficulties. But let us for the time being consider the simple case of the family in which both parents or relevant adults (or the only parent) are Christian.

COMMITMENT TO THE CHURCH

293. In such a family the parents will make their faith explicit by their open attachment to the Christian community. With religion as with most other aspects of life, those things will tend to become important to our children which are genuinely important to ourselves. If the parents' attachment to the church is marginal they must not be altogether surprised if Christianity is treated as marginal by their children. The parent who 'sends the child to Sunday school' but rarely attends church himself is effectively saying to the child: 'I think this is important for *you,* but it isn't really important for *me'.* On those terms, church and what it stands for will not in the long run be important for the child either (unless the church makes a better job of the child's Christian nurture than the parent himself is doing). We can only expect the child to make a real attachment to the Christian community if our own attachment is real. There is a reasonable chance of his finding friends there if we have friends there. He will feel at home there if we do. If he sees us responding to the demands that the church makes on our time, our money and our patience, then he will gather that the church matters to us.

294. We make our faith explicit by regularly, though not necessarily inflexibly, attending public worship. If, generally speaking, Sunday is organised round our worship, rather than leaving worship to be fitted in if it happens to be convenient when all other priorities have been met, then we

shall be proclaiming that our faith genuinely forms part of the pattern of our lives. We make the same proclamation by being careful to worship on the great festivals. But if too often the bright weather of an Easter weekend tempts us to more enjoyable pursuits than celebrating that Christ is alive after all, or if on Christmas morning it seems a shame to drag the children away from their new toys and mum from the vital task of cooking the Christmas dinner, then we shall be proclaiming something different, that giving thanks to God is just an optional extra to the other good things of life.

295. All these activities, whatever benefits we may derive from them or fail to derive, whatever virtues they may possess *in themselves* have an added significance as acts of witness. They are acts of witness first of all to the family's own members. They are a statement of priorities. Secondarily, the may be acts of witness to those outside.

296. Perhaps it needs to be said, in parenthesis, that our attitude to the church (if we are to convince our children that attachment to it is worthwhile) need to be positive but not necessarily uncritical. If we attend church regularly but spend all our time denigrating it and the other people who belong to it, our children will rightly come to wonder why we bother. But we also owe it to our children that we should be honest with them, and not disguise that fact that tensions sometimes exist within churches, that people are not always as pleasant to each other as they might be, and that church services (and other activities) are sometimes boring and unsatisfying. Our best witness consists in showing that in spite of the church's imperfections (imperfections for which we ourselves take a share of responsibility) it is the community in which and through which we come to Christ.

THE DIVIDED FAMILY

297. But this business of making worship part of the pattern of the family's life is precisely the area where the divided family faces some of its most acute problems. The Christian partner will not normally wish his faith to be divisive. To love and respect the non-Christian partner is not only his natural inclination but itself a Christian duty, and that love and respect will forbid the Christian partner's convictions. Some kind of compromise will be dictated by individual circumstances. The Christian's best witness in such circumstances is surely to show firmness in maintaining as far as possible a Christian pattern of life for himself, but not to the extent of making life difficult for members of the family who do not share his convictions. Above all, a Christian in such a position must refuse ot let himself feel guilty because he is able to spend less time in church activities than if his partner fully supported him. He is bearing witness as best he may (see paras. 260-261).

298. Not only so, but he should remind himself that according to scripture the faith of one member of a family may be effective in saving others. In Mark 9:14-29 we read how a child was healed and saved, not on account of his own faith (for he was not even conscious at the time) but not on account of his own

faith of one parent, and an only half-believing parent at that. And in a very different context, speaking of exactly the situation we are thinking of, where a Christian man or woman is married to a non-Christian partner, St Paul says:

> 'For the unbelieving husband is consecrated through his wife, and the unbelieving wife is consecrated through her husband. Otherwise, your children would be unclean, but as it they are holy.' (1 Cor. 7:14)

299. This is not to deny that there may be times of crisis and extremity when the family may become an obstacle to living the Christian life rather than an opportunity for peace and responsibility towards one's loved ones. Jesus spoke sharply about the divisions which faith in him would bring about in family life (Luke 12:51-53) and made it clear in one of his most difficult sayings (Luke 14:26) that loyalty to family must never stand in the way of loyalty to the Kingdom of God. The Kingdom transcended family loyalties and even provided the believer with membership in another, more universal, family (Mark 3:31-35). On the other hand, the healed demoniac was told to 'Go home' (Mark 5:19), several of Jesus' most memorable acts of healing restored family life broken by sickness and death: Jairus' daughter (Mark 5:35-43); Peter's mother-in-law (Mark 1:29-31); the widow's son at Nain (Luke 7:11-17). He himself blessed the marriage in Cana (John 2:1-11); was a guest in the home of his friends (Luke 10:38-42; John 11:5); and grew in grace and in favour with God and man whilst in his own family at Nazareth (Luke 2:51-52). To place the Kingdom of God above the family will not normally mean that we serve the Kingdom instead of our family. It will normally mean that the Kingdom is served by means of love and peacw with which we live in our families, even, and perhaps especially, when the family is religiously divided. If cases arise, as they may with some of the other world religions or the smaller more rigid sects, where a Christian extends tolerance to his family but is met with intolerance (see para. 131), separation may be unavoidable (see para. 130). But this step will usually only be taken when seventy times seven other steps have been taken first (Matthew 18:21-22).

Summary: The Christian family witnesses to faith by its association with the church. Where the family is not all Christian this must usually be adapted to the needs and ways of life of the rest of the family.

ATTITUDE TO THE WORLD

300. The Christian family bears witness to its children not only by its attitude to and attachment to the church as the people of God, but by its attitude to the world. This is an area in which there may be fewer problems for the divided family, for a Christian may share many values with a non-Christian partner and their attitudes to the church. What we have said so far about the Christian family may have given the impression that it is a very inward-looking thing, and that Christian nurture within it is inward-looking too. Nothing could be further from the truth. The Christian family bears witness to its own members and nurtures its own children partly through its attitude to the world. This is expressed in a number of ways.

301. First, the Christian family's attitude to the world is expressed in the judgments which its members make on issues and events. All parents make comments on items which present themselves in the newspapers, on television or elsewhere. In a Christian family these will be informed by Christian ideals and standards.

302. Second, the Christian family goes beyond mere comment and gets itself at some points actively *involved* with the world. Much of this is in very mundane ways, such as its response to charitable giving, for instance, not as a matter of putting ten pence in the box if a collector happens to come to the door, but as something to be budgeted for, along with the electricity bill and the rates, then something important will have been said about the family's priorities. Something important will have been said if the parents in some directions are seen to go beyond the simple giving of money and put time and energy into projects or organisations (other than the church) of a socially useful kind.

303. Third, the Christian family bears its witness and expresses its Christian outlook not just in its involvement with, or willingness to support, *institutional* forms of public spiritedness, but by an ordinary friendliness and neighbourliness, and an openness to other people.

Summary: The Christian family expresses faith through its critical openness towards the world and through the values of its common family life.

FAMILY PRAYERS

304. It might be said that in speaking about the Christian family's openness to the world and about its subscribing to Christian values we have moved away again from the *explicitly* Christian back to the *implicitly* Christian. Whether we regard this as explicit or as implicit Christianity perhaps depends simply on how we define our terms.

305. We are certainly moving into the area of explicit Christian nurture when we raise the subject of what one might call 'family piety'. The Christian family worships together when its members attend church together, but should there be any form of *domestic* worship or devotion? Traditionally, Christian families have practised family prayers or family Bible reading. Such practices are in sharp decline, and the decline is often regretted. It would doubtless be a fine thing if such family devotions could be restored, but to suggest that we attempt to revive them on any large scale is unrealistic. How many Christians today could attempt family prayers and family Bible reading without artificiality and excessive formality?

VARIED PATTERNS OF DEVOTION

306. There is no reason, however, why we should be bound by traditional forms as though those were the only ones available. Neither is there any

overwhelming reason why the expressions of family piety need to be regular and formal. Traditional Christian discipline has indeed emphasised the virtues of fixed and regular times of prayer, but it is precisely this demand which, in the context of modern family life, is so difficult to meet. There are many families in which it would be very hard, if not impossible, to find a time in the week when all members of the household could be relied on to be in the same place at the same time. Most of us are driven, therefore, to look for more flexible, more varied and less regular patterns of devotion. Perhaps most of us begin with too narrow an idea of what might *count* as family devotional life. There are, for example, families where it seems a perfectly natural activity to sing hymns round the piano or to a guitar. But just because it does come naturally it may not occur to them to see this activity as an expression of family piety at all. In the nature of the case, occasions for hymn-singing arise spontaneously. The idea of programming a hymn-singing slot into the family timetable is slightly ludicrous. But the lack of programming and the enjoyable nature of the exercise should not be allowed to obscure the fact that an expression of the family's common faith is what is going on.

307. There are households in which several members might watch together a religious programme on television, or listen to one on the radio. They may not think of this as a devotional exercise (particularly as they might at the same time be doing the washing up or a bit of decorating) but it *is* nevertheless a devotional exercise in the sense that members of the family are together paying attention to the things of God.

308. Similarly, television and radio programmes, news items, magazine articles, books and films of all kinds spark of discussion. In a Christian household there will be occasions where such discussion relates directly or indirectly to faith or ethics. All this, too, happens spontaneously, and again its spontaneity should not obscure the fact that in such discussions the family's faith is being expressed and its members are educating and nurturing each other in the things of God. All these things happen naturally, but if we *see* them as part of the family's devotional life we may do them a little more postively and do more to encourage them. With all these less formal or less structured expressions of piety the technique is one of seizing and improving on opportunities which naturally arise. We must not miss the point, either, that our last example, or discussions that turn to religious or moral questions, is one in which non-Christian members of the family can take part as readily as Christian ones. Such discussions are an opportunity for a sharing of views and for Christian witness.

309. Even where families are not engaging in devotional exercises in the same place at the same time, there is a feeling of mutual support to be gained from the knowledge that they are engaging in them separately. The junior school child is more likely to make use of the Bible reading notes he has been given than his big sister and his parents use similar notes appropriate to their age groups. And a ten minute quiet time before breakfast, though one is alone, is more meaningful if one knows that other people in the household do the same.

ENCOURAGING DEVOTIONAL LIFE

310. Perhaps churches could help more than they do to encourage family devotional life. A church might decide on the theme or series of themes for a given period. Biblical background to the themes might be given in Sunday school or junior church to the children, in study groups or house groups to the adults. Reflection on the themes could be prompted in numerous ways according to local conditions, and perhaps brief notes provided to stimulate thought and meditation. If such themes were well chosen they might give rise to discussion within families and across age groups. Quite apart from its effect on *family* devotional life the church as a whole should benefit from such a campaign to think about a given topic for a given period.

311. It *is* still possible to encourage and to help children, individually, to pray. Even there we need to approach the matter very carefully. We have to acknowledge first of all that non one can pass on a competence which he does not possess. We cannot teach our children to do something which we have not learnt or which we have abandoned in favour of other forms of spirituality. The fact that many Christian parents find it difficult to foster any kind of devotional life in their children is a reflection of their failure to develop a satisfactory devotional life of their own. Too often we catch ourselves recommending to our children patterns of piety which have not worked for ourselves.

312. On one thing, perhaps, we can all clear our consciences: we may doubt the usefulness of teaching children to 'say prayers' in the sense of repeating set formulae, of the 'God bless mummy and daddy and grandma and grandad...' variety. If we have failed to drill our children in such performances then probably very little has been lost, provided plenty of other opportunities for talk of and with God are created. If we think of ourselves as *teaching* children to pray we have probably already got off on the wrong foot. We cannot *instruct* a child how to pray. We can pray *for* him. We can pray *with* him. There are no other possibilities. For most of us, such is our own incompetence in the spiritual life, if we are to pray with our children we must also learn with them how to do it.

313. Meaningful prayer takes time, and reflection. It cannot be tacked on to the events of the day but must arise out of the events of the day. Perhaps the child's prayers could grow most naturally out of conversation. 'What have we done today? What good things have happened?' Think. Make a little list in one's head. The pray: 'Thank you, God, for these things.' 'What things have been on our minds today? Have there been things that roused our concern? Are there things that we are worrying about, either on our own behalf or other people's?' To bring such worries into the open is itself a kind of therapy, a healing activity. For the child, to bring his concerns openly to his mother or father and to bring them before God, are not different things, but only different aspects of the same thing. (Again we have the parent exercising his priestly office.) 'Are there things that happened today that I am sorry about?' 'Are there things that I *ought* to be sorry about?' The child might be offered the

chance to think of these privately. Even so, such occasions may become ones for confession. And parents, too, not seldom have things which they ought to confess to their children, if they could bring themselves to do so. A time of prayer conducted in the way suggested might occasionally be not only an opportunity for a mutual asking of forgiveness, but for a general sorting out of the parent/child relationship. Approached in this way both parent and child might *together* learn better how to pray. Many patterns of prayer are of course possible. This is just one suggestion. But whatever else we do, there is a great deal to be said for teaching our children the main liturgical prayers, whether it be the Lord's Prayer or the Grace or any other prayers regularly used in our churches. They should be learned and explained.

GRACE AT MEALS

314. There are other overt ways of exhibiting in a domestic context the family faith. The practice of saying grace at meals has something to commend it. It too easily becomes formal and stereotyped, and care has to be taken to avoid this. Many Christian families reserve the saying of grace to Sundays, or to the main meal of the day. This may enhance rather than reduce its significance. It is probably advisable to change the form of words at fairly frequent intervals. The saying of grace unites the family in thankfulness, which is a primary element of worship. In the saying of grace we look outward to God, not inward upon ourselves. At the same time it cannot help but remind us of those who have much less to be thankful for than ourselves, and so, to that extent, it also looks outwards to the world. The act of thanksgiving also unites us with the whole people of God in earth and heaven, for our forefathers back to biblical times have performed it. It was an old practice even in our Lord's own time. When our Lord Jesus Christ broke bread, he habitually gave thanks as he must have seen his father do.

VISUAL AIDS TO DEVOTION

315. Apart from the saying of grace, Christianity lacks traditional domestic ceremonies. Perhaps it would be helpful to build on those we have. The decoration of our homes at the great festivals might reflect our Christian convictions in better ways. Decorating the home at Christmas is normal. The Christian family can find ways to make it clear that for them it is not a purely secular occasion. At Easter the discreet introduction of a cross, or an appropriate picture, might be a practice to foster. The Catholic tradition always has encouraged the use in the home of Christian pictures or other reminders of devotion. It is perhaps to its own impoverishment that Protestantism has largely neglected such aids. They have a part to play both as a witness to those who come into the home from outside, and as constant reminders to the family's own members of the faith which they profess.

Summary: The Christian family, especially if it is unanimous, will seek for expressions of faith in domestic worship. These will vary widely and may be more informal and occasional than the older conventions.

TALKING TO CHILDREN ABOUT RELIGION

316. We have spoken of the difficulty which many parents feel about the idea of family prayers or family Bible reading. This is only one aspect of a very general problem about speaking explicitly of religious things. Religion has become one of the great unmentionable subjects of our time. It is a more embarrassing subject now than sex. Such is the climate of opinion these days that some of us *can* discuss sex with our children. Few of us find it easy to discuss faith. There is no easy answer to this problem, because the Christian, in this respect as in others, cannot insulate himself from the common current of opinion. It is no good telling ourselves that we *ought not* to find the subject difficult if the plain fact is that we *do.*

317. As with all emotionally charged subjects, we can all manage to talk about them if the conditions are right, if the subject arises naturally, and if we have the right relationship with the other parties to the conversation. What is needed, then, is a sensitivity to the occasion, and a willingness to seize opportunities when they offer themselves. Television programmes are often very useful for sparking off serious discussion of all kinds of topics. If this does happen after a late evening programme the wise parents are those who are willing to go on talking as long as their children wish to talk, however strong their feeling that it is past the children's bedtime, and maybe their own.

318. Small children, of course, are easier in this respect because they have not yet learnt to be embarrassed. They will often raise quite naturally subjects which the parent might find diffcult to raise. This is very helpful to the parent, and the parent should realise that assistance is being offered and be grateful for it. The point is that it is easier to respond to openness than to initiate it. It goes without saying that the child will not long preserve his innocence unless the parent responds with an openness similar to his own. Here, as so often, it is the child who is critically open (para. 196).

319. Naturally, children always ask the important questions just when we are busiest. This is not an accident. It is part of their well-worked out technique for getting our attention. And if we succumb to our entirely justifiable impulse to say, 'Not just now dear', or 'Ask me some other time', the child will feel aggrieved and will probably not ask some other time. Of course there are occasions when it is simply not possible to answer, but if at all possible then some sort of answer, or at least some lead towards an answer, is desirable, and may usefully be prefaced by: 'Well, to answer that properly would take a long time, but...'

320. Children rarely ask entirely frivolous questions. They often ask what seem to the adult 'silly' questions, by which we mean that they are questions

put in an appropriate form. These 'silly' questions may be among the most important which the child ever asks, and it is important not just to dismiss them. If we can show the child *why* they seem to us to be inappropriately put then something very substantial may be gained. Nowhere is this observation more relevant than in the field of religious questions.

321. The child's religious questions very frequently are explorations of religious language, though they may not at first sight appear so. Those of us who are used to it often just what a strange kind of language religious language is. Much of the language of religion and piety consists of perfectly ordinary words, but used in special senses, or used to make statements which by the ordinary rules of language are non-sensical or at least odd. The child's questions are often prompted by the fact that he has noticed this. His questions are often designed, therefore, to *test* the language of religion, to see what sort of cash value it can be given. He asks questions in order to see what *counts* as sense and nonsense in this special sort of discourse. His questions will be designed to test the religious statements he has heard, and to explore them further.

THE CHILD'S APPRECIATION OF GOD AS FATHER

322. Perhaps this can best be explained by looking at some common examples. One of the first things that any child is likely to be told about God is that God cares for him. If he ever goes to church or Sunday school he will certainly hear God described as 'Father'. Now children, even if they have no father of their own, usually have a pretty clear idea of what constitutes a father. Fathers are large, usually fairly cuddly, wear woolly jumpers and come home at about 6 o'clock. If a child moves in circles where religious language is sometimes used it will dawn on him quite quickly that God is not cuddly, does not wear a jumper and never comes in at six. He grasps the fact that when we describe God as 'Father' we are using the word in a rather special sense. We have already signalled something of this to him by using the word 'father' at all, which to the child is a *slightly* high-flown word which he meets much less frequently than the term 'daddy'. Since 'daddy' and 'father' are in most contexts interchangeable the fact that they are not interchangeable in religious contexts is significant. We call God 'Father' quite frequently. We never refer to him as 'Daddy'. The child may not articulate to himself in any conscious way but he *is* likely to sense a difference in the flavour of the two words, or at least to be feeling his way towards such an awareness.

323. The child is also aware, of course, that ordinarily speaking each of us has only *one* father, and that unless we are brothers or sisters we all have *different* fathers. So if God is a sort of *extra* father, and if all of us, regardless of parentage, can lay claim to him, then to call him 'Father' must certainly be to use the word in a special sense. Again, few children are likely to set out this argument in such a formal way, but whether they spell them out or not they are likely to be conscious of some of its implications.

118

324. This business of calling God 'Father' or referring to his care for us is just one example of a phenomenon which the child encounters constantly when his elders speak of God, their tendency to speak of him as though he were a *person*. Many questions by younger children centre round this observation and are meant to test the notion of personality; to elucidate in what respects God is, and in what respects he is not, like a 'person' as they normally understand and use that word. To the child, the most puzzling aspect of the matter is that the qualities of personality which are the most strikingly obvious to him are precisely the ones which are not predicated of God. In particular, the notions of spatiality and corporeality are troublesome, *i.e.* a 'person', as the child normally understands the term, has a body, which occupies a particular position in space and time. 'A person' can be met, and talked to. 'Persons' have places where they belong. The child gathers fairly quickly that using the language of personality with reference to God does not mean that we can see God or talk to him as we can to mummy or Auntie Jean.

325. Perhaps we ought to pause there. We have just said that 'he gathers this fairly quickly'. We do, however, in some ways make it hard for him to draw this conclusion. For one thing, traditional Bible stories often speak in terms that suggest that God *is* a person in the sense that he has a body, and occupies a particular position in space, and that he can be met and spoken to. When it becomes clear to the child that he himself never encounters God in this way, and that his parents and other adults do not talk as if they did either, he tends to resolve the difficulty by assuming that the Bible's world is a special world, different from our own, in which different rules operate. He may identify this with the world in to which he was transported in other kinds of stories. This special world of the Bible is one in which miracles are taken for granted too, as he will later learn. Many Christians never grow out of this assumption, even in adult life. If it persists it makes it impossible to have any proper appreciation of what is meant by the incarnation. For the Christian understanding of the incarnations is that it is 'in this mortal life' that our Lord came to visit us in great humility. And it has the consequence that it is 'now in this mortal life' that we must repent and cast away the works of darkness. 'Having said that, perhaps it should be added that the error has a respectable past behind it, for on it rests the old distinction between 'sacred history' – in which miracles happen and God speaks to men – and 'profane history', in which we all live and in which the ordinary, unexciting rules apply.) If the child does draw the conclusion that there is a special Bible world in which God acts more or less as other persons act then this will get in the way of his forming a more refined understanding of God.

THE DISTINCTION BETWEEN GOD AND JESUS

326. A second, very common way in which adults often make it harder for children is by failing to draw a clear distinction between the words 'God' and 'Jesus'. One hears adults say that they deliberately use the words

interchangeably when speaking to children since this makes it easier for them to understand. On the contrary, it stores up all kinds of trouble. The Bible never equates the two words and does not use them interchangeably. Moreover, orthodox Christianity has since the early centuries regarded it as a serious error to fail to make the distinction between the Father and the Son. It is of course perfectly proper in dogmatic statements to describe Jesus Christ as 'God', but it is very confusing to children to do so when making statements about the acts of the historical Jesus. It is clearer to stick to biblical terminology and describe him as God's Son, or to say that God sent him.

WHERE DOES GOD LIVE ?

327. But let us come back to the child's testing of the notion of personality as applied to God. God, he perceives, cannot ordinarily be seen and talked to. Now the only people whom the child knows about who cannot be seen and talked to are people who are a long way off, like Uncle Douglas, who has a job in Fiji Islands. But his parents talk about Uncle Douglas in ways which suggest he can *in principle* be seen and talked to. Maybe, therefore, God can in principle be seen and talked to as well. (A conclusion again suggested by Bible stories.) Maybe God *is* like an ordinary person after all, but isn't very accessible. This solution is likely to be tested by the common question, 'Where does God live?' 'Has he got a house?'

328. At this point we can illustrate some useful techniques in the answering of children's religious questions. First, we can help the child appreciate the special nature of religious language by the way in which we *introduce* the answer. To say simply: 'God lives in heaven' will appear to confirm that heaven is like the Fiji Islands, but that God doesn't often get leave. But to answer: *'We usually say* that God lives in heaven' gives the child a clue that we are using the word 'lives' in a special sense, because he knows very well that we would never tell anyone, 'We usually say that Uncle Douglas lives in Fiji'. (In Uncle Douglas' case such an answer would imply that this is what we tell our acquaintances, though the family know very well he's in jail.) The answer, 'God lives in heaven' is likely to be tested further by such questions as: 'Has he got a kitchen?' 'Does he sleep in bed?' The child is really asking: 'When you say "lives", do you mean by it what we ordinarily mean, or something different?' He suspects already that the questions don't apply. He is looking for confirmation of his suspicions. The answers will indicate that the word 'lives' is indeed being used in a special sense.

329. Instead, we might use the technique of alternative answers. This indicates that God is such a special subject that differently and apparently contradictory ways of talking about him are accepted by adults as appropriate. 'Where does God live?' 'Well, *sometimes we say* that God lives in heaven. Sometimes we say that he is everywhere.' The answer is that God is everywhere, whether offered in this fashion as an alternative, or offered by itself, makes it clear that God is only thought of as a person in some very

special sense indeed. This answer is a tough one for any child to take, and inevitably calls forth further testing. 'Is he in the airing cupboard?' 'Is he inside the piano?' Such suggestions should not be dismissed impatiently as 'silly', for they are the natural responses to the answer given, and suggest quite properly that taken at its face value the answer is so odd as to be comical.

330. Useful technique number three, which can be illustrated in answer to these supplementaries, is to offer alongside the difficult statement an indication of its practical application. Thus: 'When we say that God is everywhere, what we mean is that wherever we are we can still talk to him and he is still with us.'

RELIGIOUS LANGUAGE

331. These are simply some examples of ways in which we can assist the child to grasp religious ideas by indicating the ways in which religious language is *related to* normal language at the same time as being *different from* normal language. By this sort of answer we can show him that much religious language is analogical, and that its usefulness depends on recognising the limitations of the analogies. If we do not give the child this sort of assistance he may well conclude that religious language is to be judged by the normal criteria which we apply to everyday language, and that by this standard it is nonsense. What makes the process of answering so difficult for parents is that the child, approaching these matters with a fresh mind, notices and ruthlessly exposes anomalies which the parent has forgotten, or perhaps never come to terms with. We have to help the child to see that such extended use of language does indeed produce anomalies, and that we are aware of them, but that we nevertheless find religious statements meaningful. We have to help him appreciate that religious ways of talking have rules of their own, and to begin to show him what some of those rules are. For example, it will become clear to the child at an early stage that in religious language paradoxical statements are often acceptable, as they are not usually in ordinary life.

332. At the same time, by joining sympathetically in the child's testing of religious language we are letting him see that all religious talk is in a sense exploratory: that firm, knock-down statements are not always to be had, and that each of us has, up to a point, to develop his own religious language, guided, of course, in large measure by the religious tradition in which he stands. Thus from the earliest beginning the child should be invited to try out his religious affirmations, or those which he hears from other people, testing them against his own reason and his own experience, as well as against what he knows of his tradition. This is infinitely better than treating him to assertions, some of which he will later have to unlearn. Sooner or later, if the child is to become a Christian, he will have to make faith his own. He can be helped to do this from the start, by showing him how to *digest* religious affirmations instead of just swallowing them whole.

333. All of the foregoing has been concerned with how we respond to children's questions as and when they arise. We cannot prepare exact answers, because we do not know in advance the exact nature of the questions. We *can* prepare for the *kind* of answers we hope to give. When, in response to their questions, remarks and even jokes about religious language, our children are not met with silence or evasion, and are not reverently 'hushed' immediately back into the world of prayer and worship, but are encouraged to explore and test the meaning of the words, we will be contributing to the Christian nurture in critical openness.

Summary: In their talking about religion and in their questions, children are often testing the peculiarities of religious language. There are various kinds of reply, which have in common an intention to help the child to see the distinctive aspects of the religious words he hears and uses.

PARENTS LACK CONFIDENCE

334. Many Christian parents lack confidence. This lack of confidence shows up very sharply when they are faced by children's questions. They worry that they do not know the 'right' answers. But it is more important to give our children honest answers than 'right' answers, and we can all do that. If you are a Christian parent and your child asks a difficult question about the faith, give the answer that satisfies *you*. Say, if you like: 'This may not be the answer you would find in the books but it's the one that makes sense to *me.*' If you think it *is* the answer you would find in the books but you don't actually find it satisfying at all, then tell your child exactly that. Where the traditional answers cause problems for yourself, let your child know. It will probably comfort him, because if you don't find them easy to take, he may not either. Where there isn't any satisfactory answer known to you, say so. Admitting our ignorance is sometimes the most valuable thing we do for our children. It is important to let our children see that we think it worth going on believing, even though our faith does *not* provide complete and satisfactory answers to all questions. Faith is not a way of providing all the answers, it is primarily a way of living with the questions.

335. There is no need for lack of confidence. God himself himself has given us the job of bringing up our children. He must think we are equipped to do it. Not all of us are blessed with very great intelligence. Not all of us have had the benefits of an advanced education. But we have all been given common sense, and that is enough for most practical purposes. Jesus is saying in Luke 12:54-57 that the really important things are always plan enough to an honest mind. He ends: 'Why do you not judge for yourselves what is right?'

336. General nurture is natural. Some, doubtless, do it better than others, but once we find ourselves with the responsibility of children we find the most important things come naturally enough. Christian nurture is, for the Christian parent, an equally natural activity. If our faith is genuine at all then we find

ourselves handing it on when we lie down and rise and when we "walk by the way" (Deuteronomy 6:7; 11:19). When we allow the demands of a Christian community to help shape our lives; when Christian worship forms part of the pattern; when we let our children see that we consider prayer to be a worthwhile activity; when we answer their questions unaffectedly and honestly, when Christian standards inform the values judgments that they hear us make; and above all, when we show them the love that forgives, that can be counted on and does not need to be deserved, then we are nurturing them in a Christian way. Of course, it is worth *thinking* about these things, because if we do them thoughtfully we may do them better; but if we are Christians at all, then most of them we shall be doing anyway. Christian nurture, to the Christian parent, comes as naturally as any other kind of nurturing. This does not mean that we have nothing to learn about it, but that it 'is not too hard for you'. 'It is not in heaven,' or 'beyond the sea' (Deuteronomy 30:11-13), *i.e.* it is not an exotic, or difficult or extraneous thing.

Summary: There is no need for Christian parents to lack confidence in their attempts to nurture their children, for Christian nurture is as natural a part of the relationship between parent and child as any other aspect of the nurturing process.

GOD IS THE TRUE NURTURER

337. A further encouraging observation is that, after all, our part in nurture is a relatively small one anyway. Children grow. Parents do not *cause* that growth: it happens, like the growth of the corn in the ground, 'of itself' (Mark 4:28). This especially obvious, perhaps, in the early stages of growing. What, after all, do we actually *do* for a baby? We offer it milk at regular intervals. We change its nappy and give it a bath now and then. We smile at it and play with occasionally. None of these are, in themselves, especially exacting activities (though demanding enough to keep up, without intermission, through months that feel like years). And *that's all we do*. And yet, what our simple attentions make possible is, in those first few months, an almost explosive increase in size, skills, knowledge and an astonishing maturing of intellect. True, if we didn't feed the baby, none of it would happen, but the mere operation of inserting a few ounces of milk into the creature every four hours didn't *cause* all that, it merely enabled it to take place. Nurture is natural, but growth is mysterious; it is *given.*

338. Christian nurture is likewise an *enabling* process. Christian nurture makes Christian growth possible; it provides the conditions in which it can happen. But the real impetus for growth comes from elsewhere and is not in our hands. Paul may plant, and Apollos water, but it is God who causes the growth (1 Corinthians 3:5-6).

339. For the same reason, parents cannot decide precisely what the end product of the growth is to be. They can make sure that certain options are

available to the child, but they cannot compel him to choose them. This means that on questions of morals and faith we owe our children two things: we should let them know where we stand, and we must allow them, even if we sometimes do it with regret, to stand somewhere different if they so choose.

340. The final encouraging observation takes up a point which was made in passing several pages back (see paras. 138-141). We spoke of Christian parenthood as, in some sense, mirroring the fatherhood of God. We said that children will only grasp what the love and fatherhood of God are if they have first-hand knowledge of love and parenthood from those who bring them up. This sounds dangerous. None of us is a perfect parent. If our children know at first hand only the imperfect love that we have given them, aren't going to get an imperfect idea of the love of God? If our love is mirroring God's, then it is a highly distorting mirror. How can our children see in it any clear picture?

341. The encouraging fact is that our children do continually ˙grasp something better than we actually present them with. There comes an occasion in the life of every parent when his children will take him to task because, in some particular, they see him as falling short of the standards which he has brought them up to respect. When this happens, he should rejoice. It shows that they have grasped not his example but his ideals. It shows that they have seen through imperfections of the fatherhood he has offered them and got some sort of hold on fatherhood as it is meant to be. We observed that just by being parents and offering our children the ordinary love that parents do, we cannot help saying something about God. Inevitably we say it incoherently, fumbling, badly. Yet somehow through our incoherent words the Word itself makes itself heard.

Summary: We provide the conditions of Christian growth but we do not cause it. In the end God himself is the nurturer. Our children will catch sight of God through our nurture of them.

Chapter 15

WORSHIP AND CHRISTIAN NURTURE

346. We are not attempting in this chapter to look at all aspects of Christian worship. We are concerned only with those aspects of worship which relate to Christian nurture and growth. Neither are we attempting to prescribe how other people should worship God, or how they should encourage their children to worship God. We are looking at the way in which worship and nurture are related, and we believe that this examination has some practical implications for the way Christians should worship, but these practical implications could be worked out in many different ways. We believe that those who plan and conduct Christian worship ought to take account of the nurturing aspects of what they are doing, but how one takes account of them in the context of a liturgical tradition like that of the Church of England, for example, may be quite different from the way they are taken account of in a context of Free Church worship. (We shall return to the subject of different denominational patterns of worship in para. 364.) Worship is a nurturing activity; *i.e.* partaking in worship helps Christians to grow. Since worship is one of the central activities (perhaps *the* central activity) of the church, it would be rather odd if this were not so. Worship is the context in which much of Christian growth takes place.

347. Worship 'helps Christians to grow', but that is not the reason why we engage in worship. Worship is self-justifying. To those who know what worship is about, the question: 'But what do you want to worship God *for?'* is not one that can sensibly be asked, and certainly not one that can be answered. We do not worship God because it is good for us, but because it is 'meet, right, and our bounden duty'. Those who have met God do not ask *whether* they should worship him, or why, God is to be worshipped because he is God. He encounters us as the One who claims our devotion. (See para. 138).

348. Though we do not worship God because worshipping him brings us benefits, worship does bring us benefits, and it is his will that we should receive them. Worship involves a mutual giving and receiving. We offer to God our sacrifice of praise and thanksgiving. We offer him ourselves (Rom. 12:1). Likewise he offers himself to us. We bring him gifts. He offers us *his* gifts. And one of his greatest gifts is the gift of mature personhood.

349. These truths must not be made an excuse for placing worship beyond the reach of critical openness. It is not plausible to argue that since worship is justified simply because God is worthy of worship therefore the nurturing efficacy of worship should not be examined. For Christian life is nurtured not by any old worship we might happen to come upon or invent or inherit. Not all worship is equally good. Worship can indeed become distorted and false.

It may become a barrier between man and God. It can stunt development, actually preventing Christian growth. The kinds of worship in which we engage are determined by the kind of God we think we are worshipping, and the kind of relationship into which he calls us. Because he is not an authoritarian God who commands our service but an authoritive God who calls us into fellowship with himself we are summoned to a discriminating worship.

350. Though we do not worship God *in order* to grow, good worship (*i.e.* worship that takes proper account of who God is and what kind of God he is) does in fact stimulate Christian growth, at the same time as our maturing Christian outlook informs and reflects upon our worship. Whether we find our worship a maturing experience is therefore an indicator (though only *one* indicator) of how well we are worshipping. If we are not growing as we should, it may be that we are not worshipping as we should.

Summary: Worship and Christian nurture are linked together, in that whilst God is to be worshipped for himself alone, it is through such worship that Christian growth takes place. Worship and nurture must therefore inform and interpret each other.

THE DISTINCTIVENESS OF WORSHIP

351. Just as worship does not have to be *justified* in terms of anything else, neither does it have to be *explained* in terms of anything else. It could be said that worship is logically distinct from all other activities. Yet though it may be *logically* distinct from other activities, in practice other activities often accompany worship or are included in worship. Worship is many-sided. It might be thought of as a bundle of related activities, none of which is in itself to be *identified* with worship, but each of which may properly be *part* of worship if engaged in a worship context and in a worshipful way. These different components which may be taken up into worship are extremely varied and often contrasted.

352. We have already spoken of how worship involves both giving and a receiving, both on our part and on God's. It also involves both speaking and listening (as does any dialogue). It involves the silence of communion with God. It also involves submitting to his Word, which alerts us, judges us, teaches us, and in which we are renewed, edified, illuminated. It thus calls us to respond to the challenge of God, the challenge to amend our lives, the challenge to mission. But it invites us too to rest in the Lord and wait patiently for him. It demands that we take up our heavy cross, yet offers us an easy yoke and a light burden. It sets before us both hard commands (that we love the Lord our God with our whole heart and mind and soul and strength, and our neighbour as ourselves) and easy commands ('Take, eat'.).

353. These are only some of the elements in worship. It is thus a very rich and much-variegated experience, and rarely does any of these strands

appear alone. All this we must bear in mind as we consider a question which is vital for our understanding of the nurturing aspects of worship, namely, the relation between worship and *learning*.

Summary: Worship is a distinctive activity, unlike any other. Nevertheless, activities and experiences of many kinds may be associated with worship and be taken up into it.

WORSHIP AND LEARNING

354. To worship God is not the same as to learn about God. If, as we come away from worship we ask ourselves, 'What have we learnt?', and if the answer is 'Nothing', that does not *necessarily* mean that we have not worshipped rightly. Yet very frequently indeed, as we worship God we do learn more about him. Worship typically includes the reading, or hearing, or meditating upon God's word, and we can scarcely pay attention to God's word without learning something of his nature, the way he has dealt with men, etc.. Even if it is a word which we have heard many times before, it is always liable to strike us afresh with new knowledge and new insights. The converse is also true. Just as the worship of God and attention to his word may afford new knowledge of him, so the acquiring of new knowledge of God (*e.g.* in study or in the contemplation of his works) may move us to worship him.

355. The worship of God may bring us other knowledge than the knowledge of God himself. In worshipping God we may come to increased *self*-knowledge. We cannot face God without facing ourselves. In facing God Adam learns that he is naked (Gen. 3:8ff). In facing God Isaiah learns that he is a man of unclean lips (Is. 6:5). This is why worship is a maturing experience, because the goal to which worship moves is the beatific vision, and we cannot see God in his perfection until we ourselves are perfect as our "heavenly Father is perfect" (Matt. 5:48). The apostle expresses the same thought very clearly in 1 Jn. 3:2 when he says (speaking of the Son, not of the Father) that to 'see him as he is' and to 'be like him', are dependent the one on the other. That worship almost invariably includes the element of confession.

356. Further, the worship of God may bring with it knowledge of *others.* It is not that worship of God is likely to teach us any new *facts* about other people which we did not know before, but it may well induce us to see them in a different perspective. We cannot rightly perceive the Father without perceiving his other children as our brothers and sisters. Once more the converse may also be true. We may look at our fellows (or at ourselves) and be moved to the conclusion that all that the Bible says about human nature is true. What we learn of humanity may confirm our Christian conviction that all men need to be saved. We may also witness acts of courage or kindliness, or encounter saintly characters, which prompt us to hallow the name of God. In all or any of these ways what we learn about each other may readily pass over into prayer, praise or thanksgiving.

357. Similarly, the worship of God may bring with it knowledge of *the world*. Again, it is unlikely to teach new *facts* about the world. On the other hand, when we do learn new facts about the world, in whatever context, our refreshed understanding of the creation may well lead us to glorify the creator. And when we are struck by the beauty of the world we may respond by blessing 'the author of beauty' (Wisd. 13:3).

Summary: Worship and learning are distinct activities. Nevertheless, worship may often lead to learning, about God himself, about ourselves, about others or about the world. Conversely, learning about God may prompt us to glorify him; learning about the world may move us to praise its creator; learning about humanity may reveal our need of God and move us to repentance and adoration.

WORSHIP AND LEARNING FOR THE CHILD

358. All that has been said up to now about worship and learning applies to Christians of any age. But where Christian children are concerned there is an additional reason for not drawing too sharp a distinction in practice between the worship experience and the learning all the time in everything they do. Very many of the things they meet are still new to them. Learning is therefore an extremely prominent part of their activities and experiences. Not only so, but a substantial part of their waking hours is spent in school, and schools exist for this express purpose, that children may learn. For the child, therefore, learning is a very large portion of the business of life.

359. It is part of the function of Christian worship to give the worshipper the opportunity to bring before God his daily life, and to receive from God grace sufficient for his daily needs. When the worshipper is a child, the daily life he brings before God is a life or learning. If the child is to see the relevance of the things of God to the things of his daily life it is important to give him plenty of opportunities for *learning in the context of worship* and for *worshipping in the context of learning.*

360. For example: we may discuss with our children the regularity of the universe and its orderliness. We may explore some aspects of this order by means of simple experiments. Or we may show them pictures and charts demonstrating the development of life forms on earth. This way we do this may be very little different from the way it might be done in a physics or biology lesson at school, but the fact that these things are presented *in church,* in the context of a believing and worshipping community, and that they are accompanied by prayers for understanding and by thanksgiving for the creation will encourage the child to see them in a wholly different perspective. The same facts, the same materials may be presented, but because of the different context in which they are presented they will demand a different *response.*

361. All this is very important for the child, for he often needs help in seeing

128

how the things he learns in school for five days out of every week, and the world view which is implicit in what he is taught there, relates to the religious perspective which he is presented with on Sundays. It is not necessary that *all* of this Christian reappraisal of his secular learning be done in a context of worship, but at some point it must be brought into worship and focussed in worship.

362. Although the business of learning looms larger in the life of the child than of the adult, what we have been advocating here for the child is not different in principle from what we do in nurturing the adult. For a large part of nurturing a Christian, adult or child, is to show him how to make Christian responses to the things he already knows, and indeed, that *everybody* knows. The Christian is not someone who lives in a different world from other people, but one who lives in the same world, but interprets that world in a Christian way and responds to it in a Christian way.

363. The example given above envisaged learning in the context of worship, but it is equally important to give opportunities for worship in the context of learning. *Wherever* Christians learn together or teach each other, whether the context be called Sunday school, study group, housegroup or Christian school, opportunities should be made for a response in worship to what is being learnt; for thanksgiving for new knowledge, and for the offering of that new knowledge to God. In fact, of course, Christians generally do this almost by instinct. It seems natural to Christians to turn, however briefly, to prayer and praise in the sort of contexts which we are speaking of. This is worship in the context of learning.

Summary: Though learning and worship are distinct, children have a particular need to relate their learning to worship. It is important to provide opportunities for learning in a context of worship and for worshipping in a context of learning.

THE COMMUNITY OF WORSHIP

364. One reason why worship is a nurturing activity is that it is normally a communal activity. One might even go so far as to say that it is always and necessarily a communal activity, for when one who believes himself to be alone has thoughts of God, angels and archangels and all the company of heaven stand around him. The worshipper, even if he appears to worship alone, stands within a community, the community of faith, and the forms in which he worships will normally be the ones which his own community and its tradition have offered him.

365. When our children worship with us we are inevitably nurturing them in our own particular tradition of worship. We are initiating them into that tradition. We are encouraging them to love what we love, to share our way of expressing devotion, to find meaningful what we find meaningful. Now of course we must not speak as if our different traditions of worship are totally

distinct, or isolated from each other. That has never been the case. Each denominational tradition is part of a larger tradition of Christian worship, and the different traditions have always had a great deal in common with each other. But although this always has been the case, it is especially true in our generation that denominational patterns are being challenged by the ecumenical movement. The different streams of tradition are much less isolated from each other than they once were. Most Christian children will meet forms of worship different from the one their parents may regard as normative, and it is important to take account of this.

366. The child is very likely to experience worship in some contexts which will be inescapably ecumenical. Any worship which goes on in the school assembly of a County School ('state' school) will perforce be of an ecumenical kind. Youth Organisations of various sorts are apt to include acts of worship at some points in their programme, and these too often will be ecumenical. Further, in these days of high social mobility a child will often find himself attending a local church which may not be of the denomination in which he was earlier brought up, and may well be different from that in which his parents were brought up. For the same reasons, in many areas the local church is composed of people whose roots may be in several different denominations, and this mixture inevitably affects the style of worship, so that it may not conform closely to any one denominational pattern. This trend is affecting the Catholic church less than the others, and the ethnic congregations remain rather distinct, but most local churches both in urban and rural areas are to some degree mixtures.

367. In addition to these factors there is a much greater willingness of the denominations to accept each other and each other's ways. This leads to more frequent opportunities for worshipping in other people's churches. The same willingness has also allowed a greater frequency of inter-marriage between Christians of different denominations, so that the Christian child often inherits two different traditions from his parents.

368. The child's experience of worship will, for all the above reasons, often include an ecumenical dimension, but even where it does not, those who nurture him in the faith ought to prepare him for such ecumenical experience. They should do this by encouraging in him a *positive attitude* to other people's ways of worship. They should try very hard to avoid giving him the feeling that the way he is used to is the only proper way to worship God. They should encourage the child not to be dismissive of forms of worship with which he is unfamiliar, or which he finds at first unhelpful. In pursuit of this attempt to broaden the child's experience of worship his nurturers should give him some account of traditions of worship other than his own, and should try to help him see why some other Christians worship as they do. They should also try deliberately to find occasions on which the child may share in forms of worship different from the one to which he is accustomed.

Summary: Worship is a communal activity. The community in which the child most frequently worships will be that of his own church, and he will learn first to accept and find meaning in the forms of worship which his own church employs. But it is important that he should learn to appreciate other forms of worship employed in the wider church.

CHRISTIAN LANGUAGE

369. A large part of the business of being nurtured as a Christian, and learning to respond to experience in a Christian way, is learning the Christian language in which those responses can be expressed. To be nurtured as a Christian means to learn how Christians see things and how Christians talk about things. Worship is one of the most important contexts in which we learn this language. One of the most important kinds of Christian language is the language of worship itself. When we worship together we are not only *using* the language of worship, but by using it we are *preserving* the language of worship and *teaching* each other the language of worship. These three activities go on simultaneously.

370. Every area of human activity has its own forms of language, worship no less so than others. In mastering the activity we master the language associated with it. But today the language of worship is probably more isolated from other kinds of speech than it has ever been. In older days the language of worship borrowed many of its forms from the reverential language which was used in communicating with high earthly authorities, such as kings and potentates. It was largely 'royal' language. Today we have far fewer special forms of address for speaking to superiors. In secular contexts the earlier reverential language has largely atrophied. Secular language no longer provides models which the language of worship can appropriate, and the language of worship has no analogues outside the religious sphere. It therefore has to be learnt as a very special language, and raises particular problems for children, even where it has been modernised as far as it is possible to do so.

Summary: Worship is one of the contexts in which children acquire the Christian language. One important area of Christian language is the language of worship itself. As our children worship with us they are at the same time learning the idiom in which is done.

THE GENERATION GAP

371. It is not, however, the job of the Christian nurturer simply to acquaint children with existing patterns of worship. We have said to ourselves to the task of initiating the child into our way of worship, and the consequent attempt to look at our ways of worshipping through his eyes, may well prompt critical reflections upon our traditions of worship as they are. Nurture in worship is not rightly carried out simply by insisting that young Christians learn the ways which older Christians regard as normative. Indeed, when any such attempt

is made, the young Christians concerned are usually spirited enough to voice objections.

372. The church, like many other institutions in our society, is a victim of the 'generation gap'. By 'the generation gap' we mean the observed fact that today there are sharp cultural differences between different generations. Perhaps one of the most obvious spheres in which this cultural difference displays itself is the sphere of music. The ready availability of music on portable radios, cassette recorders etc, means that music plays a large part in the lives of many people, especially the young. And the musical tastes of the young tend to be markedly different from those of their elders. To those whose preferred musical idiom is that of comtemporary popular music the music traditionally used in church appears uninviting. The music usually found in churches is undoubtedly one of the factors which makes Christianity seem *culturally* remote to many young people.

373. Another extremely significant cultural difference between the generations is the *style of communication* to which they are accustomed. People of middle age and over received their schooling in days when it was the custom to sit children in straight rows, insist on silence, and instruct them in what it was deemed they needed to know. They were expected to speak only when spoken to by the teacher, and to leave their seats only when the teacher required them to do so. Young people have a very different experience of education. In the classroom they are accustomed to move around fairly freely, and to communicate quite freely among themselves. They much more rarely sit still and pay attention all together to class instruction. They do much more of their learning through activity. These observations at least apply to primary schools, though perhaps to a lesser extent to secondary ones.

374. Older people's experience of education is all of a piece with their experiences of church. In public worship they still expect to sit in straight rows and be silent for most of the service, speaking chiefly to make conventional responses at fixed points in the worship, or to sing hymns or psalms. They expect to remain in their seats and have someone, priest or preacher, tell them what it is they are supposed to know. Younger people, if they come to Sunday school or Junior Church, almost invariably find the same methods in use as they are accustomed to in school, for the churches have long ago adopted such methods in dealing with their children. So even on church premises they learn through activity, move around as they wish, speak freely to each other. It is hardly surprising that when we put the two groups *together* in worship we find their expectations incompatible. Worship which is satisfying for all ages can only be possible in these circumstances if a considerable amount of mutual education goes on. The different age groups have to learn to accept each other's preferred forms.

375. It is important that young Christians should learn to appreciate the traditional ways of worship, traditional expressions of Christian thought and feeling, and the traditional language of worship. Only if each generation in its

turn is prepared to treat with respect and pay serious attention to the contribution of previous generations can we maintain the continuity of the people of God and the continuity of the gospel which we preach and the faith we affirm. But, especially in a time of rapid cultural change, older Christians must be prepared for the fact that ways of expressing Christian thought and feeling which they have found meaningful and satisfactory may not be equally meaningful and satisfactory to their children. They must therefore be prepared to look for the virtues in those forms of expression which come more naturally to the young.

376. If in a Christian community we do not find this readiness to accept or to take seriously each other preferred styles, both in worship and in other aspects of community life, then the Christian nurture going on in that community is in some ways defective. Christian nurture can never be an entirely on-way traffic. We must learn *from each other* or we are not learning well. We must grow *together* or none of us will grow as we should. One of the marks of Christian maturity itself is a willingness to accept each other inspite of differences of culture. If there is in Christ 'neither Jew nor Greek, bond nor free, male nor female', then there is in him neither young nor old. If there is a 'generation gap' in our society, the church ought to be one of the places where that gap is most readily bridged. In finding ways of worshipping satisfactorily together we are both exploring and expressing our unity in Christ.

377. Although we have spoken as if the culture of the young and that of older people are two opposed and mutually exclusive systems this is not in fact the case. The cultural forms preferred by the young are by no means unfamiliar to the older generation, and by no means entirely rejected by them. To take once more the subject of music as an illustration: older people are not only familiar with popular music but frequently enjoy it *in contexts other than that of the church.* There are those who might enjoy a performance of, say, 'Godspell' or 'Jesus Christ Superstar' in the theatre, but who would strongly object to such a performance in church. They would not be objecting to the religious content, or demonstrating any inability to appreciate the music. They would rather be expressing a feeling of the inappropriateness of that particular musical idiom to the church context.

378. What this example illustrates is that the reason for the rejection by many older people of new forms of worship is not that they object to, or fail to appreciate, these forms *in themselves.* It is simply that they feel them to be inappropriate in church. Such phenomena as popular music have for them the wrong associations. Now this is a matter of cultural conditioning and with willingness and a programme of mutual education it can be overcome. We know, and are persuaded, that nothing is *in itself* inappropriate.

Summary: Some of the difficulties of worshipping satisfactorily together are due to the cultural differences between the generations. It is important that children learn to value the traditions of worship in their church. It is also important that older Christians respect the forms in which younger ones prefer to express their faith. Learning to accept each others cultural preferences is a concomitant of our growth together towards Christian maturity.

TELLING THE STORY

379. A further reason why worship is important to Christian nurture is that it is one of the contexts in which we rehearse the *story* of salvation, the story of the people of God, the story by which the people of God defines its own self-understanding. This story is of course the narrative thread which runs through the Bible, but it goes on beyond that to trace the work of God through his saints and martyrs and witnesses in every age. There was a time when this story, in diverse portions and diverse manners, was communicated in day schools, and in bedtime stories at home, and in other contexts besides. This happens less and less, and so, both for adults and children, public worship has become a relatively more important context in which the story is heard. Indeed, we may guess that for many Christians it is *only* in public worship that the story is ever heard.

380. The telling of the story, in all its various portions, is vital to the church, for it is primarily through the story that we know who we are, and who God is. When the Israelite wished to explain to his children what it *meant* to be an Israelite, he celebrated the Passover and told the story of the exodus. This story embodies two important definitions. It defines God (insofar as he is definable). Who *is* this God, the Lord, whom we worship? He is 'the Lord your God who brought you out of the land of Egypt, out of the house of bondage' (Deut. 5:6). He is defined as the God who saves, who has proved himself a saviour. And who are *we*, who call ourselves Israel? We are the people to whom these things happened. In his worship the Israelite lays claim to this story as *his* story, and therefore acknowledges this God as his God.

381. The Israelite makes the story his own by counting himself within the community of faith, whose story it is; by saying "*We* were Pharoah's slaves in Egypt" (Deut. 6:21). The story is not merely something that happened to the forefathers; every generation can use that inclusive 'we'. And the Israelite claims the Saviour as his own by worshipping daily with the words: "Hear, O Israel, the Lord *our* God is one Lord..." (Deut. 6:4). The Christian not only takes over and makes his own the story of the exodus and the whole story of old Israel, but he adds to it the story of Jesus Christ. With this part of the story the definitions are made anew. Who now is the God whom we worship? He is 'the God and Father of our Lord Jesus Christ' (1 Pet. 1:3). And we, the people of God, are redefined as those who believe in the name of the Lord Jesus Christ.

382. The Christian, child or adult, only knows who he is, where he belongs, and what has happened to him, as he hears the story of salvation and knows it for *his* story. And he needs to keep on hearing it again and again, for it never becomes so old. And worship is not only the place where he oftenest *hears* the story, but where he enters into the story, celebrates the story and becomes himself part of the story. The story is a great unifier. For when

worship centres upon the story, or (as is more usual) a particular lesser story within the total great story, it can often be shared, meaningfully, by a wide range of ages. For a story can usually be understood on a variety of different levels, and can be appreciated in different ways. Moreover, a story does not necessarily depend on every element within it being precisely comprehended. It can often speak to the hearer, and speak effectively, even when there is much in it which he does not grasp.

Summary: One of the functions of worship is to rehearse the story of salvation. When this is done effectively it can be entered into by worshippers of a wide variety of ages.

WORSHIPPING TOGETHER OR IN GROUPS

383. Whether by centring worship explicitly upon the story of salvation or by other methods, it *is* possible for Christians of all ages to worship together. In a healthy church there will be times when all members *wish* to worship together. Especially at the great festivals is this appropriate, for at such times our natural inclination is to spend less time verbalising and spelling out the meaning of our faith and to concentrate on celebrating the great acts of God. It is easy to celebrate together. It is when we attempt to verbalise that the different needs of different age groups become most manifest.

384. But Christians also feel the need very often to worship in more selective groups. Any groups of Christians will feel a ready need to worship together if they have a shared experience. (This is true even if the shared experience is of a quite short-termed sort. People who have shared a conference together, and got benefit thereby, and learnt to know something of each other in a short time, often find the act of worship with which such a conference ends a deeply moving and satisfying experience. The worship focuses their shared experience.)

385. Similarly, Christians sharing a common *work* can share profitably in worship together. Christians with a common *concern* may focus that concern in worship (as in the prayers at the meeting of the Christian Aid committee). A Christian school will naturally begin its term or its school year of life and similar situation to find benefit from bringing their common experience into worship, as a young wives group may do, for example. That such groups wish to worship and meet by themselves does not detract from their fellowship in the whole church, and no church feels a failure if some of its members thus prefer sometimes to worship in selective groups. By the same token, it should not be expected or demanded that children should *always* worship together with adults.

386. A family whose members, parents and children, *always* did *everything* together would not be regarded by most of us as normal, and would probably not be nurturing its children well. Children need the company of their peers if they are to develop normal social skills. Similarly in

135

church; the proper Christian nurture of our children *demands* that sometimes they worship in their own age group, where they can the more readily bring their common experiences, their shared concerns and interests, their desires and needs, and where they can engage in worship whose form and style is geared most closely to their propensities. In fact most worship for children is not worship in which children bring their experiences, concerns and interests, etc, before God. Most children's worship is certainly not *organised* by children. It is organised by adults, and expresses the concerns, desires and experiences which the organizing adult *thinks* the children have.

387. If our children are to learn to worship well, it is important to give them plenty of opportunities both for *involvement* in worship and for sharing in the planning and shaping of worship and for sharing in the planning and shaping of worship. Most children can in fact worship very well if given encouragement to do and say things for themselves, and given the sort of leadership which prompts them as to *possible* ways of going about it. When children do make their own prayers the adult is often made to realise how inadequate are his own attempts to lead prayer on their behalf. When children are engaging in this way in the making of worship the best leadership is that which encourages a dialogue between the children's own spontaneity on the one hand, and on the other the tradition of worship in which they are being nurtured. Children who have thus learnt in their own worship to bring before God their real joys and their real worries, to present him with their real selves and not some pseudo-self or 'Sunday-self', have a great deal to contribute when they do join in the worship of the whole family of the church, for they can lead adults too into a deeper experience of worship. Thus once more the church which nurtures its children well will find it a nurturing experience for the adult members too.

Summary: It is important that Christians sometimes worship together, adults and children. It is equally important that they sometimes worship in their own age groups or interest groups. There are dimensions of Christian worship which are more readily explored in one's own age group or interest group.

CHILDREN AND HOLY COMMUNION

388. The centre of spirituality for most Christian worship is the Communion service, the Lord's Supper or the Mass. The relation of the child's spirituality to that of the Eucharist must be considered. We need to ask whether preparation for this sacrament should take place outside it or within it. We need re-examine the conditions governing who shall be present and who shall participate. Where would the child be placed if we emphasised the difference between actual communication and communication of intent, or a spiritual and inward communication? By what means are the images in this worship conveyed to the worshippers? How important is understanding and how damaging is misunderstanding? Are there acceptable alternative

actions for children (*e.g.* the blessing) and how strong is the case for making use of any such? Is there a 'readiness' within Christian nurture for participation or presence at Holy Communion and if so how can it be fostered and recognised?

389. One of the reasons for the renewed interest in the question of children and Holy Communion is the desire and requst of Christian parents. Many parents want their children to be with them during the service as an expression of Christian family identity. It is thought that this would not only recognise and strengthen the role of the family in Christian unbringing but would also help to establish Christian identity through the idea that children in the church standing within the sphere of the address of the Gospel have a special privilege and responsibility which other children appear not to have. We do not speak of 'non-Christian children' (paras. 215, 219) but we do speak of Christian children to whom much is evidently given and from whom much is rightly demanded. The intimacy of the home is the proper context for the family agape on Maundy Thursday, and perhaps the special 'communion meal' every Sunday, but such domestic celebrations are much stronger and more significant to all the family, underlining the truth that the family is also a church if there are links with the eucharistic worship of the whole congregation. This will be one of the points at which denominational traditions may have to be modified in the light of a new understanding of the nature of Christian nurture.

390. The following criteria are relevant to the admission of children as participants in the Eucharist. We do not all attach equal importance to each criterion, and it may be that a child need not, in every case, meet every criterion. We also recognise that current policy in some of the churches is against admission of children to Holy Communion, and that therefore what we suggest would not always be feasible even if our arguments were thought sound. Nevertheless, these are, the relevant pastoral considerations.

(a) The child should be part of a Christian family. His parents or other caring adults must be fully agreeable and indeed the initiative may perhaps come from them. This is important so that the Christian nurturing process, given impetus by the communion service, will be continued in the child's own home.

(b) The child should be baptised or offered other recognised initiation by the church so that his process of Christian growth is explicitly sealed as being the responsibility of the church. Normally this will take the form of Holy Baptism, but in the case of churches in which infant baptism is not practised, it is enough if some form of dedication or offering of the child with and by his parents is performed. The vital thing is that the church should have accepted responsibility for the Christian nurture of the child, and that this acceptance should have been presented before the congregation so as to symbolise, present and seal God's calling of the child to grow in grace.

(c) The child must show evidence that he is ready. Here the testimony of wise and responsible parents who have been advised by experienced fellow Christians will carry considerable weight. It is not inappropriate to use such

137

traditional language as asking if the child manifests signs of grace, in attending public worship, in showing an interest and a love for the Christian faith, in a way suitable to his years, and some readiness, displayed not only in a degree of understanding of the Christian story, but his other reactions to the story. The assessment of this responsiveness and readiness of the child would be done informally through consultation. The child's own personal desire to communicate would be important.

(d) There should be some sort of preparation, whether through a period of attendance and observation, or through being told the story of the last supper, or through some other preparation as judged suitable to the needs and aptitude of the child and adequate by the church.

391. The idea of the rights of the child, especially his spiritual rights, has an important place in this discussion. The child has a spiritual right to use the framework provided by his religious upbringing or to reject it. He has the right to express his spiritual awareness but should not be forced to. He has the right to participate in the spirituality of his own tradition or to seek another. He has the right to make his faith and his desire for growth public but he must not be intimidated into doing so. On the other hand, the church also has the right of discriminating and of testing. These rights must be kept in balance.

We commend these criteria for consideration by the churches. Clearly if such criteria were agreed and met, then the right of the Christian child to participate in the Eucharist would be established.

Summary: If certain considerations are taken into account children have the right to partake in Holy Communion.

APPENDIX I

CHRISTIAN NURTURE IN CHRISTIAN SCHOOLS

392. In 1977 in England and Wales one child in eleven attended a Catholic school (although once Catholic child in three did not). When we add the considerable numbers of children attending Church of England schools and those of other denominations, it is clear that the education offered in such schools is of great national importance. But here we are concerned with the role of such schools in providing Christian nurture.

393. The time seems ripe for a reconsideration of their distinctive contribution to Christian growth. As with the school system as a whole, the time of expansion seems to be over, and there is now the opportunity of directing the energy which went into that expansion towards greater control of Christian quality. Moreover, some of the factors which exercised a distorting effect upon the church schools in the past are no longer as important e.g. denominational suspicions or the withdrawal tendency of threatened communities.

394. The renewed interest in ecumenical or inter-church schools can be seen as a mark of this re-thinking. At present there are some half dozen such schools, and others are in process of formation. They are partly the product of practical considerations, such as the declining birth rate and the falling school rolls, and partly due to the ecumenical inspiration which finds an opening in such circumstances. Such ecumenical schools may become a significant feature of the school system in years to come, and may provide new opportunities for Christian nurture.

EDUCATIONAL ADVANTAGES OF CHRISTIAN SCHOOLS

395. The special contribution of these church-related schools can be seen partly by contrasting them with the general state school system. The values of the public democracy, enshrined in the 'common' school, may usefully be balanced by a certain amount of protection for the ideological groups which make the pluralism what it is. The rich pluralism of the common life can be enhanced by such special schools, provided that they are outward looking. In cultural as well as educational terms, the Christian schools serve this purpose, if we think of Christianity or even specific denominations as being cultures or sub-cultures. It may also be the case that where a child's school forms one milieu with his home, his place of worship and other institutions particular to his culture, the child is less likely to become alienated from his school, and so more likely to succeed educationally. Of course, it is also true that a school may be Christian in some ways while remaining 'common' in others e.g. by cutting through racial or social barriers. The Christian schools have in general welcomed comprehensivisation, and this supports the view that they combine common and Christian elements.

396. Indeed, the church school might even operate, as many Church of England schools have done, a policy of being open to non-denominational or non-Christian pupils, and without any proselytising intentions. Such a policy would reflect a sense of Christian obligation towards the wider community, plus the belief that the Christian school has more than simply its faith to offer to the young, a belief e.g. that the special 'warmth' of Christian schools can do something to counteract the anonymity of city life.

397. Considerations of this kind are reasonable contributions to public discussion of education. They are made possible by the fact that the Christian spokesman for the Christian school himself accepts the values of the educational ideals of the common school system. On the other hand, such observations might well be acceptable to the non-Christian parent or educator, without at all moving him to send his own children to Christian schools. This suggests that these educational advantages, even allied with their helpful implications for Christian nurture, do not represent the inner heart of the Christian schools.

CONTRIBUTIONS TO CHRISTIAN NURTURE

398. That heart has normally been a combination of the two following rationales (a) the Christian schools are believed to possess a strategic advantage over the other Christian nurturing agencies, such as the 'Sunday Schools', when it comes to the denominational or the general Christian growth of pupils. (b) They are thought to possess an educational advantage over the secular schools in that they appreciate certain educational values which are very much a part of the Christian vocation, although not in themselves peculiarly Christian. These would include love of others, and sharing with others, love of creation for itself and not for what can be made with it or done with it (see para. 138), and a hope which is able to withstand the most realistic acceptance of evil. This second rationale does imply some criticism of the philosophy of education which is thought to actually prevail in the secular schools, a criticism of it as a philosophy.

399. These aspects of the Christian nurture offered by the church schools may be considered both in relation to the schools' work in religious education, and also their general curriculum. The religious education in the Church schools, although not wholly identifiable with Christian nurture is certainly not to be thought of as being in tension with it, and inasmuch as Christian nurture certainly includes an instructional element, this may be better learned by the pupil if he experiences it spread out over his school week than if it is all concentrated into a Sunday morning or afternoon. We may surely also trust that it will be better done by the professionally trained teachers in the day school.

400. The church school will also contribute to Christian nurture through its 'hidden curriculum', where because of the distinctive atmostphere, partly the product of the school life of prayer and worship, and because of the

socialisation of pupils into friendship and even marriage with one another, an invaluable contribution will be made to the building up of non-institutional aspects of church life. We may also believe that such church schools will lay emphasis upon the common human values associated with 'love', and that although they will obviously have no monopoly on these values, they will be concerned for them with a deliberation which one might not find in the ordinary schools.

401. It also should be the case that the general curriculum in the church schools can contribute to Christian nurture, and in such a way that the proper autonomy of the school subjects will not be infringed. This will be so when there is, within the Christian school, a belief in Christian culture and Christian humanism. One would expect to find a greater sensitivity to the sort of religious issues which may and should arise in teaching literature, music and history, an additional perspective on health and moral education, and a greater importance attached to community studies and problems of third world development. More profoundly, it might be reasonable to expect that where the issue is the *point* of history, science and the disciples in general, the Christian school will be more likely than other schools to consciously adopt the stance of open rationality that was outlined in paragraphs 135-137. The subjects are to be acknowledged in their own nature as objects of beauty, goodness, wondrousness and importance and also against the satisfaction and the ethical requirements of the intellectual life. This stance is not specifically Christian faith, hope and love. So it would not seem unreasonable to expect that a Christian school will lean instinctively towards this view, even when it does not actually profess it, and will do this with more assurance than the normal secular school.

CRITICAL OPENNESS AND THE CHRISTIAN SCHOOL

402. Thus there are advantages for Christian nurture in the strategy which places the child in the Christian school as well in his church on Sundays. But will the Christian school be likely to lose the vital element of critical openness? Since Christian nurture can be conducted with critical openness in the family and church, it can surely retain this when it is associated with religious education in schools. Moreover, since critical openness is demanded by the very nature of Christian nurture, this demand will be greater not less when taking place within a church school, in which Christian grounds for learning are bound to be influential. This must be insisted upon, since although indoctrination is not necessarily part of church school life, it is likely to be a greater hazard when Christian nurture embraces school as well as family and church than when Christian nurture in family and church is balanced by a wholly secular religious education in a county school. It cannot be denied that church schools have often succumbed to this temptation, to the detriment not only of their educational work but their Christian nurture as well. We think therefore that church schools should bend over backwards a little in this area. Such schools must be very sensitive indeed to the pupil's

freedom of conscience, including his or her right to opt out in varying degrees and ways both for a time and permanently. There must be no sanctions, either formal or informal, obvious or subtle. The authentic Christian nurture of the Christian school can only be the richer for offering this freedom. This approach is not recommended as a promising tactic but rather as a basic principle of faith and of intellectual conscience.

403. The role of critical openness and free enquiry are further underlined when we remember that in the Christian school where religious education and Christian nurture may become closely associated the content of the teaching will be rather broader than it will be when Christian nurture is confined to teaching on Sunday. For the church can take for granted as being provided by the school that which the Christian school must actually provide. This would apply to an understanding of religions other than Christianity and of world views other than religious ones. Not only must the Christian school ensure this breadth of curriculum, but it may perhaps develop a different approach to world religions from that of the secular school. As well as the purely educational tasks of imparting information, understanding and evaluation of religions, it can also aim for the kind of open hearted dialogue in faith, an encounter of religions which enriches faith, for the conversation between religions can be heard from the inside.

404. The view of critical openness which we have outlined may provide a bridge linking the religious educational and the Christianly nurturing aspects of this part of the curriculum. The world religions, including Christianity, would on this approach continue to be open to the pupil who wished for a purely educational encounter with them; indeed, the general context of Christian nurture in which such study took place in the Christian school could, on our view, deepen the spirit of enquiry and the seriousness of the study, thus forming a better education as well as a sounder Christian nurture.

THE WITNESS OF A CHRISTIAN SCHOOL

405. The Christian nurture which takes place in the church and in the Christian family is, in a sense, a private matter for Christians. But the Christian nurture which takes place in the Christian schools, especially when these are voluntary aided schools (i.e. closely related to the state school system) is open to the public view and in important respects answerable to the public. Here the vision which we have been describing must touch the actual realities. Are all Christian schools friendly and non-authoritarian? How many of them give priority on their curriculum to developing an awareness of the problems of the Third World? Surely many church schools lag behind some state schools in this, as in the other matters. Does the criticism of the philosophy of the curriculum implied in one aspect of the nature of the Christian school (see para. 403) really apply? There are, after all, Christians teaching in state schools, and many teachers who although not Christian share a similar view of the nature of the curriculum and of the world. There can be

no denying the fact that often the secular school will be serving the human and educational values better than the Christian school, although the latter has Christian reasons for prizing them. The image of Christ may be found more clearly in the secular school than in the Christian school. A measure of humility and a readiness to learn seems appropriate for the church schools at this point. This spirit of humble listening (critical openness) is consistent with Christian confidence and with the obligation laid on the church schools that they should be a witness to the secular schools.

406. On the other hand, the witness of the Christian schools must be robust. Not only will the Christian nurture they offer to their pupils be nobler, but the service rendered to the secular schools will also be enhanced. Of course there is no value in merely being an alternative to the state school system. But let there be schools which in their teaching and their structures explicitly and implicitly allow the light of the Christian gospel to seach the value assumptions alternative. They will constitute a challenge to the state schools which naturally reflect the wider values of modern thought and life, and they will also be allies of the state schools as the latter confront the very values they cannot but reflect. For example, surely all schools are charged with the task of criticising materialism and consumerism. They are all bound to help pupils to distinguish the joy of creativity from the pride of possession. Similarly, all schools must value and respect childhood and youth, in themselves and not merely as a preparation, and this respect must extend with special carefulness to the children who are deprived, the handicapped, the lonely and the disturbed.

407. Difficult although it is, all schools have a duty not to be intimidated by scholastic orthodoxies and academic disciplines, to realise that even these 'sabbaths' are made for man and not man for them, to humanise the curriculum without sacrificing humility before the truth. No school can be complacent about the extent to which it fulfils these obligations. This is partly because no one is sure exactly what their full and detailed implications might be for the curriculum and the structure of the school. But the Christian school should be in a favoured position to begin to realise all this, provided it has the courage really to think through the implications of such New Testament emphases as authority conceived of as service and not as domination, the centrality of compassion, the respect given to childhood, the idea of spiritual poverty, or the Pauline insistence on mutual encouragement and on the freedom of the sons of God.

408. These then are some of the ways in which the Christian schools might contribute to Christian nurture, and in doing so might form a bridge between Christian nurture and Christian mission. They are advantages of the Christian schools from the point of view of Christian nurture and not arguments for the church schools as such. There may be other reasons for these schools and other arguments against them. Not all church schools need be dedicated to Christian nurture, and there are also things to be said for the secular county school as well, even from the point of view of Christian nurture. *The Child in*

the Church report did not deny that Christian nurture could properly take place in county schools. It did deny that the county school had 'any more responsibility in principle for Christian nurture than for the nurture of Muslims, Jews or Humanists' (Recommendation 12). We also suggested (Recommendation 14) that 'what might be appropriate for Christian nurture in church schools be investigated'. This Appendix has been a response to that reflection. We have not devoted attention to Christian nurture in the secular schools, partly because that would have led us into many wider and more complex fields, and partly because our task has been to examine the nurture of the child in the church.

RECOMMENDATIONS

Note: The following recommendations are directed towards the improvement of the nurture of the Christian child in the Church. Each recommendation, although it may raise other questions which lie beyond the scope of this Report, should be interpreted in the light of our major concern, Christian nurture. Most of the recommendations are discussed or implied at various stages of our Report, but some of the more closely connected paragraphs are indicated after each recommendation.

A. ADULT EDUCATION (See also recommendations 6 and 8)

1. **Leadership**
   We recommend that the Churches should give greater priority to the training of resource persons, both ordained and lay, who will be able to offer effective leadership in nurture.
   Paragraphs 5(a), 20, 124.

2. **Clergy education**
   We recommend that all clergy education, whether ordination or in service training, should include as an essential component the study of Christian nurture.
   Paragraphs 20, 120.

3. **Parent education**
   We recommend that local Churches give greater attention to parent education (1) including especially the Christian understanding of the Bible (2) modern Christian thought (3) psychology of children (4) and the practice of the Christian faith in the home (5)

   (1) Paragraph (1) 5(e)   (2) Paragraphs 74-87, 26(b)
   (3) Paragraph 26(a)   (4) Paragraphs 17-20, 92
              (5) Paragraphs 39-40, 112-115

4. **Ecumenism**
   Since a great deal of work in training personnel and providing teaching materials goes on in separate denominations, and since we believe such work would benefit greatly by sharing insights, we recommend that local Churches and councils of Churches make every effort to see that such work is undertaken in an ecumenical context.
   Paragraphs 5(a), 16(c), 69, 105-6.

B. THEOLOGY

5. **Theology of nurture**
   We recommend that, since the renewal of the Churches' ministry in nurturing both children and adults requires for its support a theology which sees critical openness as springing from Christian commitment,

145

the attention of the British Council of Churches Division of Ecumenical Affairs to be drawn to this area of theological construction. Paragraphs 23-26, 44-69, 73.

6. **Study outline**
We recommend that a study outline on the place and significance of childhood in the Christian faith be prepared for use by local Churches with groups of parents and other adults. Paragraphs 28-43, 95.

C. DEVELOPMENT OF KNOWLEDGE AND RESOURCES

7. **Research project**
We recommend that the churches establish an ecumenical research project in order to discover, initiate and disseminate experimental work in the nurture of the child in the Church. Paragraphs 5(f), 6, 92.

8. **Christian Learning Resources Centres**
We recommend that the Churches examine the possibility of further development of a chain of Christian Learning Resource Centres on an ecumanical basis. Paragraphs 5(b), 15, 16(c), 20.

D. THE CHILD AND THE ADULT CONGREGATION

9. **Christian initiation**
We recommend that in the necessary re-examination of their various initiation ceremonies the Churches should bear in mind that children in the Church are not to be thought of as being in a stage of mere preparation for the Christian life nor as being merely in preparation for adult membership. Paragraphs 5(d), 34-38, 41-43, 66-67, 93-100, 118.

10. **Worship: integration**
We recommend that since children should be more clearly seen to be part of the worshipping community churches should give careful consideration to times, places and patterns of worship in order to effect the appropriate integration of children and adults. Paragraphs 5(c), 70, 91-100, 115-124.

11. **Worship: participation**
We recommend that gatherings of the local Church for worship should be modified so that greater opportunity is created for the participation of children in ways appropriate to them and to the liturgy. Paragraphs 5(c), 13-14, 20, 21, 91-100, 115-124.

E. SCHOOLS

12. **L.E.A. Schools**
We recommend that since the L.E.A. school can no longer be expected to carry any more responsibility in principle for Christian

nurture of Muslims, Jews or Humanists, local Churches must accept full responsibility for the Christian nurture of their young. Paragraphs 22, 88, 109(f).

13. **Religious Education**
We recommend that the local Churches should explore ways of building upon the work done by the L.E.A. school in its provision of an open, descriptive religious education into a variety of religions, realizing that there is no necessary tension between such religious education and the goals of Christian nuture. Paragraphs 22, 51-52, 110.

14. **Church schools**
We recommend that the church schools should explore and express the distinctions between religious education and Christian nurture. In particular, what might be appropriate for Christian nurture in church schools be investigated. Paragraphs 49-64, 112, 108.

NOTE AND FURTHER RECOMMENDATIONS
Chapters 8 to 15 are an attempt to respond to some of the above Recommendations made in 1976, particularly Recommendation 5, which asked for some work to be done on the theology of Christian nurture, Recommendation 9 which suggested that the nature of the child as a member of the church should be taken more seriously, and 10 and 11 which asked for a greater recognition of the Christian child as a participant in church worship. Recommendation 4 said that Christian nurture should be an ecumenical and not a denominational activity, and we have tried to incorporate this not only in the content and outlook of the later chapters but in our own ecumenical composition as a small working party. We would like to draw attention to the remaining Recommendations, of which some have received attention but others refer to situations and problems in which there seems to have been little change since 1976. Chapters 8-15 have not sought to make a popular appeal and we still think there is a need for a simplified study outline for more general use in the churches, as envisaged by Recommendation 6. We understand that the United Reformed Church will publish a pack of leaflets for this purpose in 1984.

15. **Moral Education**
There are certain areas needing further study. One is the moral education of the Christian child, or the nurture of the Christian child in Christian ethics. The relativism and plurality of the open society have quite sharp impact upon traditional Christian moral values, and while there has been a great deal of re-thinking for Christian adults, we are not aware of very much that deals with morals in the context of the sort of Christian nurture which we advocate.

16. **Christian Curriculum**
    A second area of possible investigation is Christian curriculum, especially for the teaching which takes place on Sundays in churches, but also for Christian schools. We have not been a curriculum working party, but we think that the view of Christian nurture outlined above might be used to discriminate between various kinds of teaching material now being used in the churches, and it might even give rise to some new emphases in curriculum for Christian learning (see para. 138).

17. **Children and the Sacraments**
    We have ventured some observations about the child in Holy Communion. We are aware that much more needs to be done in this area, and that the child's place in the other sacraments and ordinances of the church also needs further study.

18. **Literature for Parents**
    Our discussions about Christian parenthood made us aware of the need for suitable literature for the guidance of the parent who is not a church member of even religiously inclined, but does not want his children to be deprived of the benefits and enrichments of the religious life. We think that a leaflet on religious education in the home which did not adopt a moralistic or an evangelistic approach towards the parents but offered practical suggestions about stimulating the religious experience of the child in the broadest sense would be welcomed by many families which are secular and yet not opposed to religious insights.

BOOK LIST

J. Sutcliffe, **Learning and teaching together,** NCEC

David P. O'Neill, **What do you say to a child when you meet a flower,** Anthony Clarke Books

Janes W. Fowler, **Stages of Faith,** Harper & Row

J. Westerhall, **Will our children have faith,** Seabury

Hans Rudi Weber, **Jesus and the Children,** WCC

ed. C. Herbert, **Dear Adults,** CIO

J. Klink, **Your child's religion,** SCM

MEMBERS OF THE WORKING PARTY FOR PART I

Rt. Rev. John Gibbs
(Chairman)

Bishop of Bradwell, former Principal Keswick Hall College of Education.

The Rev. Philip Cliff

Chaplain & Head of the Deparment of Church Education, Westhill College of Education.

Deaconess Anne Dixon

Assistant Director of Education in Durham Diocese.

Mrs. Barbara George
(from January 1974)

Head of Religious Education, Gumley House School, Isleworth. Roman Catholic.

Miss Jean Holm
(from July 1974)

Head of Religious Studies, Homerton College, Cambridge.

Dr. John Hill

Lecturer in Education, School of Education, Birmingham University.

The Rev. Rodney Matthews
(resigned December 1973)

Former Director British Lessons Council Church Education Curriculum Development Project. Minister in local Baptist Church.

The Rev. David P. Munro

Church of Scotland minister. Chairman, Church of Scotland Board of Education.

The Rev. Dr. Henry McKeating
(from July 1974)

Lecturer in Theology, University of Nottingham. Methodist minister.

The Rev. Krister Ottosson

British Council of Churches Secretary Education Unit, Division of Community Affairs.

Mr. John Nicholson
(resigned January 1974)

Warden, Southwark Diocesan Conference House, Adult Lay training Officer Southwark Diocese.

Miss Beryl E. Underhill

Secretary for Children's Work Training, Methodist Church Division of Education and Youth.

The Rev. John Pridmore

Chaplain — King Edwards School, Witley. Formerly — Chaplain and Tutor Ridley Hall Theological College.

The Rev. T. Carlisle Patterson
(resigned November 1974)

General Secretary Conference of British Missionary Societies.

The Rev. John Sutcliffe
(from May 1974)

General Secretary Christian Education Movement. Formerly Secretary

Education Dept. United Reformed Church.

Miss Rosemary V. Wilcock
(Secretary)

Staff member Church of England Board of Education.

MEMBERS OF THE WORKING PARTY FOR PART II

The Right Reverend John Gibbs, who was chairman of this Working Party and also the *Child in the Church* Working Party, is Bishop of Coventry. He was Principal of Keswick Hall College of Education in Norwich from 1964 to 1973 and Bishop of Bradwell from 1973 to 1976.

Dr John M. Hull is Senior Lecturer in Religious Education in the Faculty of Education of the University of Birmingham. He has been Drafting Secretary and Editor of this report and of the *Child in the Church* report. He has been Vice-Chairman of the Christian Education Movement since 1971 and is editor of the *British Journal of Religious Education*. His books include *Hellenistic Magic and the Synoptic Tradition* and *School Worship, an Obituary*. He is a layman of the United Reformed Church.

Dr Henry McKeating is a Senior Lecturer in Theology in the University of Nottingham where he specialises in Old Testament studies. He is a member of the Divisional Board and also of the Executive Committee of the Division of Education and Youth of the Methodist Church and Chairman of the same Board's Education Development Committee. His publications include *God and Guilt, God and the Future, Amos, Hosea and Micah* (in the New Cambridge Bible Commentary) and *Studying the Old Testament*. He is a Methodist minister and was a member of the *Child in the Church* Working Party.

Reverend David F. Tennant is Head of the Church Education Section of Westhill College in Birmingham and Secretary of the Birmingham Council of Christian Education. He is a member of the Baptist Union Education Committee and the Education Committee of the Free Church Federal Council. He is the author of *Children in the Church: A Baptist View* and a contributor to "All Generations, a Handbook for leaders of Family Worship". He is a Baptist minister and a member of the BCC Consultative Group on Ministry Among Children.

Mr Patrick D. Walsh is Lecturer in Curriculum Studies in the London University Institute of Education. Previously he was lecturing in philosophy and religious studies at St Mary's College, Strawberry Hill. He is presently working on two books dealing with an 'alternative' philosophy of education. He is a Roman Catholic layman.